ACCLAIM FOR CARMEN AGUIRRE

"Aguirre's writing is splendid; she combines black humour and a sharp intellect and tells her powerful story in grand style."

—*Publishers Weekly*

"Aguirre writes like someone who knows how it feels to exhale with no certainty that another breath will follow."
—*National Post*

FOR *CHILE CON CARNE*

"Carmen Aguirre's witty, semi-autobiographical monologue about growing up as a refugee of Chile's Pinochet regime vividly captures the feelings of a child torn between two worlds."

—*The Globe and Mail*

FOR *¿QUE PASA WITH LA RAZA, EH?*

"When we think about the culture of *Las Américas, con acento,* Canada rarely comes to mind. However, the recent moving premiere of *¿QUE PASA with LA RAZA, eh?* by the Latino Theatre Group, located in Vancouver, British Columbia, on both the cultural and geographical map of *Nuestra América.*"

—*Theatre Journal* (U.S.)

CHILE con CARNE

& OTHER EARLY WORKS

ALSO BY CARMEN AGUIRRE

*Blue Box**

Mexican Hooker #1 and My Other Roles Since the Revolution

Something Fierce: Memoirs of a Revolutionary Daughter

*The Refugee Hotel**

*The Trigger**

*PUBLISHED BY TALONBOOKS

CHILE CON CARNE

& OTHER EARLY WORKS

THREE PLAYS:

In a Land Called I Don't Remember

Chile Con Carne

¿QUE PASA with LA RAZA, eh?

CARMEN AGUIRRE

Talonbooks

Talonbooks
278 East First Avenue, Vancouver, British Columbia, Canada V5T 1A6
talonbooks.com

Talonbooks is located on xʷməθkʷəy̓əm, Sḵwx̱wú7mesh, and səl̓ilwətaʔɬ Lands.

First printing: 2018

Typeset in Arno
Printed and bound in Canada on 100% post-consumer recycled paper

Cover design by Roberto Cortez and Peter Riddihough
Interior design by andrea bennett

Talonbooks acknowledges the financial support of the Canada Council for the Arts, the Government of Canada through the Canada Book Fund, and the Province of British Columbia through the British Columbia Arts Council and the Book Publishing Tax Credit.

LIBRARY AND ARCHIVES CANADA CATALOGUING IN PUBLICATION

Aguirre, Carmen, 1967–
[Plays. Selections]
Chile con carne and other early works : three plays / Carmen Aguirre.

Chile con carne – ¿Que pasa with la Raza, eh? – In a land I don't remember.
ISBN 978-1-77201-228-6 (SOFTCOVER)

I. Aguirre, Carmen, 1967– . Chile con carne. II. Aguirre, Carmen, 1967– . Que pasa with la Raza, eh? III. Aguirre, Carmen, 1967– . In a land I don't remember. IV. Title.

PS8601.G86A6 2018 C812'.6 C2018-905026-8

In memory of Manuel "Manelo" Delgado, Ana Maria Espinoza, Nelson Rodríguez, and Jaime Villaseñor, founding members of the Vancouver Chilean community in exile, elders, teachers, mentors who formed me. All gone before their time, in the 1990s. These plays were written in the context of their passing.

A lost country lives within me
Like an enemy it appears in my dreams
As if a forgotten sea were banging on my chest
And the life I already lived
Appeared before my eyes.

—INTI-ILLIMANI, "CUECA DE LA AUSENCIA"

CONTENTS

PREFACE

All three plays in this collection were written in the 1990s, when I was in my twenties.

At that time, new plays about the Canadian immigrant experience often performed gratitude to the mainstream, essentializing the mythical, exotic country left behind as static and undeveloped and Canada as advanced, rational, flexible, and superior. It seemed that these plays wanted to cater to the new Canadian Multiculturalism Act, a government effort to contain radical demands to end racism. I wanted to inhabit the public sphere by telling stories about refugees of colour, with content that was anti-racist, anti-capitalist, and anti-imperialist. Performing rituals of my culture so that the mainstream could see that I too am human was of no interest to me. First and foremost, I wanted to take up public space for my own community.

When I started theatre school in 1990 at the age of twenty-two, I had no idea I would end up doing any of this. That seems preposterous to me now, but when I began my acting training I thought that those in the theatre wouldn't see I was a brown refugee. Naively, I was under the false impression that the arts world lived outside of society in a kind of utopia where systemic racism and other "isms" were not only kept at bay but fought against. I was wrong. Within six weeks of my first semester, I was told by the faculty that in my acting profession I would only ever play hookers and maids due to my race. Was I sure I wanted to continue with my training? As shocking and humiliating as this information was, it propelled me to create my own work while still in school. It was there that I decided to tell the stories of the Latinx community in Canada, from my point of view as the child of Chilean political exiles.

Being raised in exile is different from being raised as an immigrant. Immigration is all about reinventing yourself in a new land; exile is about the triumphant return to the homeland. Exiles are unwanted both in their motherland and in the new country. Growing up in an uprooted state leads the child into chronic cultural identity crisis.

I wrote my first play, a political thriller entitled *In a Land Called I Don't Remember,* at the age of twenty-five, while I was still a student. It premiered at my school, Studio 58, in March of 1995, a year after I graduated. The piece explores the theme of exile through two characters who are the same age: Claudia and Ana Maria. Claudia is returning to Chile for the first time; Ana Maria has always been there. They sit next to each other on the bus that will take them across the Andes from Argentina into Chile. It is July 1986, and the assassination of Pinochet is being planned. In *In a Land Called I Don't Remember,* I investigated both sides of my cultural identity through these two characters. Claudia is returning to the home she barely remembers, while Ana Maria, a Resistance member, is giving her life to the cause. Everyone at Studio 58 assumed that the character of Claudia was based on me. The opposite was true: I had just returned from having spent four years in the Chilean Resistance. This play, like almost all my work, is unabashedly left wing.

Chile Con Carne, a dark comedy, also premiered in 1995. It was the first time in professional Vancouver theatre history that an autobiographical one-woman show explored exile and internalized racism from the point of view of an eight-year-old child. The play was written as a response to the assumption that children are not affected by exile because quite often they can't remember their homeland, are able to pick up the new language without a trace of a foreign accent, and quickly integrate into the mainstream. Immigrant and exiled children are bicultural – monocultural in both their cultural settings. Because they are chameleons, it would appear that neither one of their cultures questions what's going on inside the child's mind. *Chile Con Carne* is an attempt to give those children a voice. It continues to receive productions in Canada, and has been presented in Chile and Venezuela in translation.

In a Land Called I Don't Remember and *Chile Con Carne* both examine memory and culture clash. Both were written shortly after the end of the Pinochet dictatorship and the Cold War, when left-wing content was considered an artistic risk in Canada, due to fear of alienating the audience. In each of these plays I investigate how to present violence in the theatre without being exploitative, morbid, or shocking. It is a question I continue to probe in much of my work.

¿QUE PASA with LA RAZA, eh? is one of the most fulfilling theatre experiences I've ever had. Based on the lives of members of Vancouver's Latino Theatre Group, it was co-written with some of them when I was in my late twenties and they were in their mid-to-late teens and early twenties. The Latino Theatre Group, formed in 1994 through Headlines Theatre Company (later Theatre for Living), where I was working as a Theatre of the Oppressed workshop facilitator, was made up of non-actors from Vancouver's Latinx community. As facilitator of the group, I offered a series of theatre games and exercises designed to enable the participants to share their stories of oppression, thus transforming them into stories of resistance. In 1999, after presenting over twenty-five original short Forum Theatre plays at different events around Vancouver, we premiered *¿QUE PASA with LA RAZA, eh?* at the Firehall Arts Centre. It was a culmination of six years of gathering stories, working and reworking scenes through structured improvisation that was then written down, developing six protagonists, finding a structure – in short, devising a brand-new play based on the lives of the people on stage. *¿QUE PASA with LA RAZA, eh?* also deals with exile, trauma, culture clash, and poverty. It too is unapologetically left wing. In the 1990s, the majority of Vancouver's Latinx population (one of the poorest demographics in the city at that time) was made up of refugees fleeing right-wing state terrorism. For the first time in Vancouver theatre history, a full-length, original play tackling this subject matter was created and presented by a group of non-actors from the Latinx community on a professional stage. The play was nominated for a 1999 Jessie

Richardson Theatre Award for Outstanding Artistic Achievement. The Latino Theatre Group ran until 2002, and its members credit it with changing their lives.

As I go back and reread these plays, I am moved and inspired by the youthfulness of the writing. Sometimes I cringe at the lack of skill, but more often I am proud that a left-wing, young refugee woman of colour managed to write and co-create three new plays for an audience that was dying to see itself onstage. None of it would have been possible without my training at Studio 58, without my Latinx community, my family, my fellow artists, without the support of our federal, provincial, and municipal public funding bodies. I am forever grateful for the opportunities that I have had and for the determination of that young woman who insisted on doing her work on her own terms, no matter what stood in her way.

IN A LAND CALLED
I DON'T REMEMBER

PRODUCTION HISTORY

In a Land Called I Don't Remember was developed at Studio 58 in Vancouver, British Columbia. It was produced there from March 22 to April 2, 1995, as part of Studio 58's inaugural FourPlay festival, with the following cast and crew:

CLAUDIA	Tracey Erin Smith
ANA MARIA and secondary characters	Cyndi Mason
MANUEL	Anthony F. Ingram
BUS DRIVER and secondary characters	Dean Paul Gibson
DOÑA MARUJA and secondary characters	Laurel Lemley
DON FERNANDO	Stephen Holmes
DON MARTIN	Jonathan Teague
PLIN PLIN and secondary characters	Jonathon Young
LUCHO and secondary characters	John Gordon
LA GRINGA	Judi Closkey

Director	Jane Heyman
Dramaturge	John Lazarus
Set & Lighting Design	Ross Nichol
Costume Design	Sarah Armstrong
Sound Design	Attila Clemann
Design Assistant	Terence van der Woude
Stage Management	Krista Mennell

CHARACTERS

The twenty-one characters in this play can be performed by ten actors.

To be played by one actor:
ANA MARIA, age nineteen
LITTLE SISTER, age four

To be played by one actor:
CLAUDIA, age nineteen
CLAUDIA, age five

To be played by one actor:
LUCHO, age twenty
GARCIA, age thirty
SECRET POLICE #1, age twenty-seven
SOLDIER #2, age eighteen

To be played by one actor:
BUS DRIVER, age thirty-five
FATHER, age thirty

To be played by one actor:
DOÑA MARUJA, age sixty-five
NANA, age sixty
DON FERNANDO, age sixty-seven
DON MARTIN, age sixty
MANUEL, age twenty
LA GRINGA, age thirty

To be played by one actor:
CAMPOS, age twenty-nine
SECRET POLICE #2, age twenty-five
SOLDIER #1, age eighteen
PLIN PLIN, age thirty

SETTING

The entire play takes place on a bus. It is essential that an atmosphere of claustrophobia be created. During all scenes, all characters are busy chatting with one another, eating, drinking mate, carrying out other activities, resting, even if the focus is not on them. These activities are not always written into the script.

SCENE ONE

Note: The last song to be played during walk-in, leading right into Scene One, is "Cueca de la ausencia," by Inti-Illimani.

July, 1986. The bus station in Neuquén, Argentina.

BUS DRIVER walks on and starts preparing the bus.

DOÑA MARUJA and DON FERNANDO arrive. BUS DRIVER loads their things, takes their tickets, and they settle onto the bus.

LUCHO and ANA MARIA arrive. They embrace and kiss. (Note: This embracing and kissing is an act for anyone who may be watching. These two characters are not lovers – they are comrades in the Resistance.)

DON MARTIN arrives.

"Cueca de la ausencia" fades out.

LUCHO: (*secretly, into ANA MARIA's ear as they embrace, referring to her suitcase*) Did you sew it into the lining?

ANA MARIA: No. I'd rather have it on me.

LUCHO: Better to go down with the boat.

BUS DRIVER: (*to ANA MARIA, LUCHO, and DON MARTIN*) Good morning, I'll take your bags.

MANUEL arrives with his guitar and other belongings. ANA MARIA and LUCHO break their embrace.

BUS DRIVER: (*taking ANA MARIA's suitcase*) Valdivia?

ANA MARIA: Yes.

BUS DRIVER loads DON MARTIN's and MANUEL's belongings while the following interaction happens inside the bus:

DOÑA MARUJA: (*wiping off his shoulders*) Look at this! The kids are going to think we were caught in a snowstorm in the middle of the Andes! Have you been using those herbs I boiled for you? Doña Reina said they'd get rid of your dandruff quicker than a spell.

DON FERNANDO: It's dust, woman. You didn't brush off this suit.

DOÑA MARUJA: Where's your head? I spent hours getting that suit ready. I borrowed Doña Luca's brush – oh, my saint, I forgot to give it back! I left it on the wash basin –

Outside the bus:

BUS DRIVER: (*to MANUEL, who is strumming a* cueca *on his guitar*) You taking that guitar on my bus?

MANUEL: 'Course I am.

BUS DRIVER: You got a good voice?

MANUEL: Sweeter than a church choir.

BUS DRIVER: Okay. No protest shit, though.

MANUEL: Hey, we're still in Argentina, a free country, and I'll sing what I please.

BUS DRIVER: Not on my bus you won't.

MANUEL: You live in Chile?

BUS DRIVER: Yup.

MANUEL: Somehow that doesn't surprise me.

BUS DRIVER: Got my family waiting in Valdivia with some fresh fish, ready to throw on the stove. (*to ANA MARIA, LUCHO, MANUEL, and DON MARTIN*) I'll take your tickets!

ANA MARIA: (*whispering to LUCHO, as they embrace*) Don't worry about me. In a month, it'll be all over the papers and you'll know we succeeded.

DON MARTIN: (*inspired by MANUEL's guitar playing, breaking into a* cueca *dance with ANA MARIA, while LUCHO, DON MARTIN, DOÑA MARUJA, and DON FERNANDO whistle, laugh, and clap*) When to Chile I go, the *cueca* I dance with a beautiful girl. She hides behind her hanky –

CLAUDIA enters.

CLAUDIA: Wait!

The guitar playing, singing, and dancing stop.

CLAUDIA: Please! (*referring to her backpack*) I gotta get this loaded!

BUS DRIVER: Hand it over, Miss. (*taking the backpack*) Holy shit! What do ya got in here? Bombs?

CLAUDIA: No.

He loads the backpack and moves to the door of the bus.

BUS DRIVER: Let's go. Hand me your tickets!

*The passengers get on the bus. ANA MARIA sits at the window of the first seat, in front of DON FERNANDO and DOÑA MARUJA. She waves goodbye to LUCHO. He waves back and exits. DON MARTIN sits across the aisle from ANA MARIA, and MANUEL sits at the very back, strumming his guitar. CLAUDIA, carrying her leather daypack and her magazine (*Time *with a picture of Tom Cruise on the cover), is the last passenger to get on the bus.*

CLAUDIA: Excuse me, I was wondering if we could possibly ... um ... would you mind ... um ... you know ... uh ... would you mind trading seats with me?

ANA MARIA: Sure.

CLAUDIA sits in the window seat. ANA MARIA takes the aisle seat right next to her.

CLAUDIA: Thanks. I'm Claudia Cortez ... I really want to look at the view, that's why.

ANA MARIA: Oh. You're not gonna see much.

CLAUDIA: Why not?

ANA MARIA: 'Cause there's a snowstorm.

CLAUDIA: Oh, well ... they can't be as bad as the ones in the Rockies.

ANA MARIA: Uh-huh.

CLAUDIA: You know ... the ones in North America. In Canada, the States.

ANA MARIA: Yeah, yeah. I've looked at a globe before.

BUS DRIVER gets the bus moving.

BUS DRIVER: We're off! (*crossing himself*) In the name of the Father, the Son, and the Holy Spirit. Amen.

CLAUDIA: (*under her breath*) I hope this piece of shit makes it through the snow storm. Think we'll make it?

BUS DRIVER: Stop that! You'll put a curse on my bus!

CLAUDIA: I hear the route we're taking is a lot like where I live ... Vancouver ... on the west coast.

ANA MARIA: You don't look Canadian.

CLAUDIA: I wasn't born in Canada, but I am Chilean Canadian.

ANA MARIA: Oh, come on! Make up your mind! Either you're chicha or lemonade!

CLAUDIA: I'm chicha. Valdivia to be precise.

ANA MARIA: Valdiviana!

CLAUDIA: You too?

ANA MARIA: Born and raised.

CLAUDIA: I was there till I was five – till the coup happened –

DON MARTIN: Saving of the fatherland.

CLAUDIA: Do you know the Martinez family? The mother taught history at the Andes University.

ANA MARIA: Martinez? No, no Martinez there.

CLAUDIA: Oh, it doesn't matter. That was years ago anyway. Are you a student?

ANA MARIA: Second year.

CLAUDIA: What are you studying?

ANA MARIA: History.

CLAUDIA: Wow. I don't know if this is an ignorant question, but I thought history was banned in Chile.

ANA MARIA: That was a while ago.

CLAUDIA: Right! After the coup!

BUS DRIVER: Saving of the Fatherland.

ANA MARIA: Things have changed.

CLAUDIA: You mean that if I wanted to, I could study history or psychology or philosophy in Chile?

ANA MARIA: 'Course you can.

CLAUDIA: I'm lucky I ran into you. I'm thinking of going to university there.

ANA MARIA: In Chile?! Don't tell me there's no good universities in Canada!

CLAUDIA: Yeah, but it wouldn't be as exciting.

ANA MARIA: As exciting as what?

CLAUDIA: As studying in a place where there's so much going on. Where the youth are so active in standing up for their rights, where huge changes are taking place, and the people, knowing they have nothing more to lose, are grabbing the regime by the balls and –

ANA MARIA: Shhh.

CLAUDIA: What? Oh. (*in a whisper*) I just want to see for myself what goes on there, I've heard enough speakers talking about the situation, and seen too many documentaries. I'm also becoming really active in the Solidarity with Chile Committee –

DOÑA MARUJA: The gringos have a committee for us?

CLAUDIA: I'm sorry?

DOÑA MARUJA: What's this committee all about?

CLAUDIA: Well, it's not just gringos, it's Chileans also. We raise money for the families of the disa –

DON FERNANDO: Hell! I've never seen any of that money! Who gets the money? I'll bet Pinoshit gets all the money!

DON MARTIN: Pinochet.

DOÑA MARUJA: (*to Don Fernando*) Shut that degenerate mouth of yours and let her finish! (*to Claudia*) Go on, my treasure, he's just drunk.

CLAUDIA: Oh, okay. Well, we raise money for the families of the disappeared and –

DON MARTIN: Disappeared? What the fuck are you talking about? There are no disappeared in Chile! Those are lies made up by international communism to give the General a bad name! Fucking lies! All your so-called disappeared are sunbathing in the Caribbean, laughing, as their families raise the roof with stories of midnight raids and mass graves. Lies! All fucking lies!

ANA MARIA: Yes! Thank you. Who wants a butt?

BUS DRIVER: Over here!

DON FERNANDO: I do!

DON MARTIN: Hand one over!

CLAUDIA: I think I'll have one too.

ANA MARIA: Smart move.

DON MARTIN: Lies. Communist lies.

CLAUDIA: (*coughing*) Woah! These are strong!

DOÑA MARUJA: What do you know about the disappeared?

CLAUDIA: Well, that there's at least twenty-five hundred of them –

DOÑA MARUJA: Dear God, the Virgin Mary, and all the Saints.

DON FERNANDO: Twenty-five hundred? Where did you get that number?

CLAUDIA: Well, I mean, doesn't everybody know that? It's in the media and –

ANA MARIA: (*grabbing CLAUDIA's* Time *magazine with Tom Cruise on the cover*) The media? You mean along with Tom Cruise?

CLAUDIA: No, I didn't mean that kind of media –

ANA MARIA: But he sure is cute, isn't he? Well, let's just see what *Time* has to say about world events.

CLAUDIA: (*grabbing magazine back*) Stop that!

ANA MARIA: So you have the hots for Tom. Can't blame you! Healthy, blue-eyed American boy, dropping bombs over the Middle East for his Uncle Sam –

CLAUDIA: Well, obviously you like him enough to have seen *Top Gun*.

BUS DRIVER: Hold on tight! There's a sharp curve!

DON MARTIN: Need a hand with the driving, boss?

DON FERNANDO: Yeah, we're right here for you, boss.

BUS DRIVER: Nobody drives my bus but me.

DOÑA MARUJA: (*to CLAUDIA*) Are you travelling all alone, my dear?

CLAUDIA: Yes.

DOÑA MARUJA: Where are your parents? Why didn't they come with you?

CLAUDIA: Oh, they wanted to, but they're on Pinochet's blacklist.

DOÑA MARUJA: My Lord. They must be worried sick about you! It's dangerous ... all alone ... the military will know when they look up your name ... we'll all take care of her and make sure she gets home safe and sound, right boss?

BUS DRIVER: Absolutely. That's my job.

CLAUDIA: Thank you. That's very kind of you.

BUS DRIVER: Oh, it's not just me. The good spirits show me the way.

DOÑA MARUJA: How big do you think Chelito will be?

DON FERNANDO: Oh, about so high. I bet you he'll be strong, too. Takes after me that boy.

CLAUDIA: I thought the disappeared was common knowledge –

ANA MARIA: Good for you, wise woman.

CLAUDIA: Look, I've heard about the mass protests, about the Mothers of the Disappeared getting organized. Even the Church speaks out against the atrocities!

ANA MARIA: Have you heard that forty percent of the country kisses Pinoshit's ass?

CLAUDIA: No way.

ANA MARIA: How do you think he stays in power?

CLAUDIA has a memory of PLIN PLIN, the clown who would come on Chilean National Television every night before bedtime.

PLIN PLIN: I am very sad today, children. This is a very sad day for our country. Have faith, be strong, and fight. One day you will walk in freedom again.

A military march comes on.

Back on the bus.

DOÑA MARUJA: (*handing CLAUDIA some bread*) Oh here you go, my dear. So young and all alone! It's fresh out of my oven.

MANUEL, who has been strumming his guitar throughout this scene, starts singing. As the song progresses, more people join in, until everybody is singing.

MANUEL: *Cambia lo superficial,*
cambia también lo profundo,
cambia el modo de pensar,
cambia todo en este mundo.
Cambia el clima con los años,

cambia el pastor su rebaño,
y así como todo cambia
que yo cambie no es extraño.

Cambia todo cambia × 4

Pero no cambia mi amor
por más lejos que me encuentre,
ni el recuerdo ni el dolor
de mi pueblo y de mi gente.
Lo que cambió ayer
tendrá que cambiar mañana,
así como cambio yo
en esta tierra lejana.

Cambia todo cambia × 8

MANUEL: (*holding up a bottle of wine*) Here's to a safe return!

DON FERNANDO: Here's to the tyrant's fall!

DOÑA MARUJA, MANUEL, CLAUDIA, DON FERNANDO, and ANA MARIA (*though ANA MARIA not as passionately as the rest*): And he will fall! And he will fall! And he will fall! And he will fall!

DOÑA MARUJA: And to the end of exile!

DON FERNANDO: I'll drink to that!

MANUEL: Maybe this year!

DOÑA MARUJA: Let's keep on praying.

DON MARTIN: Ah, you people just don't remember what it was like before the Saving. At least now, it's safe to walk on any street in Chile. No fear of delinquents.

DOÑA MARUJA: How would you know? You live in a shantytown here in Argentina!

DON MARTIN: I came here, drawn by all this talk of the new democracy in Argentina. Well, see where democracy has gotten them? There's no work, the youth are lost in drugs and delinquency, and we're treated worse than the Indians here.

DON FERNANDO: He's right!

DON MARTIN: If this is democracy, I'll take the General any time. That's why I'm going back. No more shantytowns for me!

BUS DRIVER: Hang on tight! Sharp curve again!

ANA MARIA: (*to BUS DRIVER*) How long till we get across?

BUS DRIVER: Judging by the snow, I'd say about thirty-six hours.

ANA MARIA: You're jokin' with me.

BUS DRIVER: Serious as a saint. I'm surprised they haven't closed down the roads.

ANA MARIA: This is gonna be torture.

DON MARTIN: But at the end of the road we'll be in Valdivia! Ah, I can already smell the air.

CLAUDIA: Is it really gonna take thirty-six hours?

BUS DRIVER: Yup. What are you doing way down in the ass of the world?

DON FERNANDO: Yeah, what are you doing in this shit hole?

DOÑA MARUJA: You're a disgrace! I'm sorry, dear, he gets like this when he drinks –

DON FERNANDO: If I was in Yankee-land, I'd never set a foot down in this place again!

The bottle gets passed around.

CLAUDIA: Uh, excuse me, Canada is a separate country, nothing to do with the States.

BUS DRIVER: It's true. My neighbour's cousin is exiled there. Sends postcards sometimes. Of Edmonton.

CLAUDIA: Edmonton? Wow. And to answer your question, I think Chile is the most beautiful place on Earth.

DOÑA MARUJA: She's right. When God finished creating the world, He had all these little leftovers: pieces of deserts, volcanoes, mountains, rivers, lakes, seas, and valleys. He didn't know what to do with them, so He threw them over His shoulder. All these bits and pieces landed in the remotest corner of the world. That's how Chile was created.

CLAUDIA: (*fumbling with her Walkman*) Oh, please say that again, I'd like to record it.

ANA MARIA: (*under her breath*) Make me puke.

DOÑA MARUJA: When I remember my country, I stop in my tracks and weep like a widow. Anything can start it: a smell, the sound of a child laughing, a bit of wine, and there it goes. When you're in exile, it's best not to remember.

DON FERNANDO: I'd say it's best for you not to drink wine, old lady.

DOÑA MARUJA: Look who's talking.

CLAUDIA: At least you have something to remember.

DOÑA MARUJA: You must remember something if you say it's the most beautiful place in the world.

CLAUDIA: Yeah, I guess. I don't know if what I remember is real or imagined.

DON MARTIN: Well! You'll soon see for yourself! Chile has never been better. You feel safe there. And people are polite. Not like these dirty Argentinians –

BUS DRIVER: Hey! Shut up! Argentinians give me a lot of good business!

DOÑA MARUJA: People are scared!

DON MARTIN: And they should be! With all those Marxists blowing up buildings, robbing banks –

MANUEL: American banks.

DON MARTIN: Cutting off the electricity! They're trained by the Cubans. I say the General should stop trying to please everyone and get rid of the terrorists once and for all!

DOÑA MARUJA: There's no terrorists in Chile. All those bombs are planted by the military themselves to give them an excuse to kill innocent university students.

DON MARTIN: What do you mean there's no terrorists? Hell, I know what I'm talking about! Let me tell you something. Back in '70 I got involved with the Reds. They brainwashed me into believing that we'd have peace if we fought imperialism, or so they called it. Well, they lost their fight, thank God and the General for that, and now they want revenge at any cost.

DOÑA MARUJA: Don't be an imbecile. I don't know why I even bother talking to a shameless drunk. As if my husband weren't enough!

MANUEL: (*to CLAUDIA*) Welcome to this fucking country.

MANUEL strums his guitar.

Time passes. ANA MARIA sleeps.

MANUEL: (*approaching from the back of the bus, mate and thermos in hand, to CLAUDIA*) So. I hear you're from Canada.

ANA MARIA wakes up as MANUEL settles into the seat next to theirs.

CLAUDIA: I wasn't born there.

MANUEL: Home is where you hang your hat.

CLAUDIA: Or where the heart is?

MANUEL: I don't know about yours, but mine is pounding away nicely inside me.

CLAUDIA: I'm Claudia Cortez.

MANUEL: I'm Manuel. And this is?

ANA MARIA: Ana Maria.

MANUEL: Manuel.

ANA MARIA: (*referring to the mate*) That Argentinean yerba?

MANUEL: Yeah. Best you can find. Here.

CLAUDIA: I think I'll pass, thank you.

MANUEL: You don't know what you're passing up.

BUS DRIVER: I'll have some!

MANUEL: (*passing the mate to BUS DRIVER*) People in Chile kill for Argentinian yerba.

BUS DRIVER: (*after having drunk it and passing it back*) Aaah! Hits the spot!

MANUEL: (*preparing another one, to CLAUDIA*) Come on, did he die from it? It warms your insides.

CLAUDIA: This is mate, right?

ANA MARIA: Yeah, what did you think it was? Drugs?

CLAUDIA: It's like tea, right?

ANA MARIA: (*grabbing the mate from MANUEL*) Goddamn it woman! Just try it!

MANUEL: Don't move the bombilla! You'll ruin it!

CLAUDIA: (*trying some*) God, that's bitter!

ANA MARIA: The cigarettes: too strong! The mate: too bitter! Wait till she tries the men!

CLAUDIA: Okay. Give me a cigarette.

MANUEL: Ooohoohoo! I think I'll have one too. (*after lighting up his cigarette*) So. What are you doing here?

CLAUDIA: Well, this is my first time in Chile in thirteen years.

MANUEL: You shoulda just taken a plane.

CLAUDIA: No way! I heard that crossing the Andes is magnificent!

MANUEL: Try it on foot some time.

CLAUDIA: On foot?

MANUEL: Yeah! That's how I came to Argentina. Gotta do it in the summer, though.

CLAUDIA: How long did it take you?

MANUEL: Oh, a couple of days. It's faster on a mule, but I was broke, so I walked. It's my first time back, too. I left on February 10, 1983. I'll never forget it. I can't believe more than three years have already gone by!

CLAUDIA: I take it you were forced to flee Chile.

MANUEL: You could say that. It would have been nice to go to Canada, though. How did you manage that?

CLAUDIA: We went as refugees. We got asylum.

ANA MARIA: You don't look so bad off. For a refugee.

CLAUDIA: You should have seen us when we first got there. My parents went from being professors to janitors. Did you get refugee status in Argentina?

MANUEL: Refugee what? I came here with the clothes on my back. Full of hopes, what with the new democracy coming and all. I'm lucky I wasn't deported. Now I have a work permit.

DON FERNANDO: And how long did it take you to get it?

MANUEL: Three years.

DON FERNANDO: Ha! Took me two!

DOÑA MARUJA: *Mijito!* You're worse than a child! Competing with the boy!

MANUEL: It hasn't been what I expected, but I can't complain. Do you live in Argentina too, Ana Maria?

ANA MARIA: No, no.

CLAUDIA: Ana Maria lives in Valdivia. She studies history there.

MANUEL: Valdivia. I'm from Pucón. But I used to have family in Valdivia.

DON FERNANDO: For two years I got up at five in the morning to stand in lineups, but they finally gave me my permit.

MANUEL: My uncle and aunt were found floating in the river in Valdivia.

CLAUDIA: Floating in the river?

MANUEL: Found by some kids. Barely days after the coup. My uncle was a fisherman. They accused him of hiding arms in his boat. One day he didn't return. That afternoon they kicked the house apart and dragged my aunt away. Neighbours say she screamed and scratched like an alley cat. My little cousins got home from school and all they found was the kettle boiling on the stove. We took care of our cousins after that. In Pucón. I'll never forget when they arrived at our house, in their Sunday best, Yani with ribbons in her hair, her eyes red from crying.

BUS DRIVER: Hold on! Curve!

ANA MARIA: The only time I cried was when Plin Plin said goodbye.

BUS DRIVER: Now I must admit that was sad.

CLAUDIA: Plin Plin! That's his name! Plin Plin!

ANA MARIA: You remember him?

CLAUDIA: Yes, yes! I was just thinking about him! The Clown Plin Plin! He lived in a box and would get up and teach the children how to brush their teeth.

ANA MARIA: Eight o'clock on the dot. National TV.

MANUEL: Shit, man. My family never had a TV. Are you talking about that clown that disappeared?

BUS DRIVER: Vanished into thin air. I cried when he said goodbye.

CLAUDIA: Yeah! Me and my sister cried too.

BUS DRIVER: I'll never forget Plin Plin crying, fading away, a military march coming on.

DOÑA MARUJA: Not even in Chile yet and already it's coming back to her! Oh, the mind is a wonderful thing! I'm sure your parents would have been so happy to share this moment with you! I can't imagine being on a blacklist, not being able to step on my own soil.

MANUEL: Why do the pigs have them on the list?

CLAUDIA: To break them.

DON MARTIN: What did your parents do?

CLAUDIA: They were university professors, they did political theatre and literacy in the shantytowns, they had people over all the time, singing and dancing into the night.

DOÑA MARUJA: So they were good people who enjoyed life.

CLAUDIA: Yeah, but they changed so much after the – Saving. They talked in hushed voices, with the curtains drawn tight. Once, I woke up in the middle of the night. I crawled out of my bed, halfway down the stairs, and there were my parents, on the living-room floor, huddled in each other's arms, my dad crying ...

my parents still don't know I saw them that night. They don't like to remember those times.

BUS DRIVER: I guess when you're far away you don't want to be reminded every day.

MANUEL: How did your family manage to get to Canada?

CLAUDIA: I don't know. They never told me how. I just remember not saying goodbye and packing very few belongings, leaving Valdivia behind. What was it like growing up in Valdivia?

ANA MARIA: Quiet. Wet. Boring. Isolated.

CLAUDIA: I can't wait to get there. I can't wait to get home.

DOÑA MARUJA: Neither can I, my dear, neither can I.

CLAUDIA remembers PLIN PLIN again.

PLIN PLIN: And now, boys and girls, it's time for a story, so gather 'round. There once was a little girl who went for a walk in a land called "I Don't Remember." She spent much time walking, and when she tried to find her way home, she found that she was lost. She took two steps here and two steps there, but with every step she took, she was more lost than before.

SCENE TWO

Night time. ANA MARIA and CLAUDIA are covered by a blanket. They talk in quiet voices. The rest of the passengers are sleeping.

ANA MARIA: You got a boyfriend?

CLAUDIA: Yeah, his name's Richard.

ANA MARIA: Wow!

CLAUDIA: What?

ANA MARIA: That's an exotic name!

CLAUDIA: Oh!

ANA MARIA: I'm so used to guys being called Antonio or Rodrigo ... Richard ... I like the sound of it ... What does he look like?

CLAUDIA: He's gorgeous.

ANA MARIA: I've always wondered what it would be like to be with someone totally different. Like a gringo.

CLAUDIA: Yeah, well, I don't know if he's really a gringo. (*showing ANA MARIA a picture*) See?

ANA MARIA: Oh my God, he's Black! Where's he from?

CLAUDIA: Canada.

ANA MARIA: I didn't know there were Blacks in Canada!

CLAUDIA: His family has been there for six generations.

ANA MARIA: (*studying the picture*) Wow! Nice body!

CLAUDIA: Tell me about it. I miss him like hell. It was only a few days ago when we said goodbye, but, man, it seems like forever.

ANA MARIA: How long have you guys been together?

CLAUDIA: Two years. We met in high school.

ANA MARIA: Two fuckin' years! I can't hang on to a guy for more than a month!

CLAUDIA: Why?

ANA MARIA: Oh, after a month I always realize that no matter how progressive, they still want the little woman to take their shoes off for them at the end of the day.

CLAUDIA: Jerks.

ANA MARIA: It's the women who are idiots. They let their men treat them like shit.

CLAUDIA: Not me.

ANA MARIA: Me neither. I just can't seem to find a guy who's as good about the politics as he is in bed.

CLAUDIA: Well ... I guess a good fuck is better than nothing.

ANA MARIA: Of course. But you seem to be getting more than that. Two years with this Richard!

CLAUDIA: Yeah. I'd been eyeing him for a whole year, and finally, right before we graduated, we got together. It was totally scary. It took balls to ask him out.

ANA MARIA: You mean *ovarios.*

CLAUDIA: Oh, yeah. It took *ovarios.*

ANA MARIA: You asked him out. Just like that.

CLAUDIA: Sure. I thought, "We're graduating in two weeks! There's no time to waste!" So I called him up and asked him if he wanted to go to a Chilean dance with me. It was the hottest night of my life.

ANA MARIA: Holy fuck! I wish I could do that!

CLAUDIA: Just do it. The worst thing that can happen is he'll say no.

ANA MARIA: Right. Then I get labelled "Slut of the Student Union." In Chile, you gotta make people believe that the guy's making all the moves and you're just going along with it. Otherwise, not only the men, but also the women will tear you to shreds, honey.

CLAUDIA: Okay, so you make them believe that, but you still ask him out. I mean, just think if he says yes!

ANA MARIA: No, no. He'd be in a state of shock at a sister making a move.

CLAUDIA: Who is this backward guy?

ANA MARIA: José Godoy de la Cruz; he's four years older than me.

CLAUDIA: Okay, so he's not an adolescent, he can handle a little *ovarios* from a sister, I mean, like, does he know you exist?

ANA MARIA: Yeah, I went into the Student Union 'cause he's one of the leaders. I'd seen him around. Painting "Students Resist" on the walls. On the riverbank with the other Student Union people. I'd watch him clean his spectacles as he listened to one of the others, run his hand through his curls, sigh deeply and say "*compañero*." I ached for him to call me *compañera*, so I joined.

CLAUDIA: And after all your political commitment he hasn't warmed up to you.

ANA MARIA: He's taken.

CLAUDIA: Shit.

BUS DRIVER: (*referring to another curve*) Hold on!

ANA MARIA: We necked once, but he pretends it never happened.

CLAUDIA: Typical.

ANA MARIA: Far from it: we had no choice but to neck.

CLAUDIA: You had no choice?

ANA MARIA: A military pig had come from Santiago to give a talk at the university, so we were having a protest. Tear gas, truncheons, rubber bullets. José was in charge, and part of the plan was that we'd break into small groups if we got trapped. And guess who I ended up running down an alley with?

CLAUDIA: José Godoy de la Cruz.

ANA MARIA: Exactly! Anyway, we're holding hands, tearing down this alley. We can barely breathe – 'cause of the tear gas – and we're weighed down by our bags full of rocks and pamphlets calling for the uprising of the masses. We run like crazy till we get to a plaza, and just then a jeep rounds the corner, full of military pigs, looking for us. We tore our handkerchiefs off our faces, flung ourselves on a bench, and before I knew it, I had him straddled, with my tongue down his throat. We heard the jeeps screech on by. The pigs thought we were lovers, nothing to do with the protest.

CLAUDIA: Well!? Did you just keep making out?

ANA MARIA: No! As soon as the jeep was gone I got such a big laugh attack I just about pissed my pants, and he started looking around in a daze. He made me swear over my dead grandmother not to tell his girlfriend, Rosalia.

CLAUDIA: You've just had the hottest moment of your lives and he's worried about the girlfriend? It's like, relax bud.

ANA MARIA: The worst thing is I've become good friends with her.

CLAUDIA: Shit, that changes things. Does she know you humped him on a bench?

ANA MARIA: What?! You want me killed?

DOÑA MARUJA: Do you girls want another blanket?

ANA MARIA: No, we're fine.

DOÑA MARUJA: Well, if you need anything I'm right here.

CLAUDIA: Thank you. We're fine.

DON FERNANDO: Leave the poor girls alone, woman! Goddammit!

CLAUDIA: Do you guys have lots of protests?

ANA MARIA: Yeah. We're pretty organized.

CLAUDIA: Has anything ever happened to you?

ANA MARIA: What are you asking?

CLAUDIA: Have you ever been ... I don't know ... in jail or something?

ANA MARIA: Why do you want to know?

CLAUDIA: I want to know what I've missed.

ANA MARIA: You make it sound like you weren't invited to a party.

CLAUDIA: Sometimes I feel that way.

ANA MARIA: That's pathetic.

CLAUDIA: What's so pathetic about it?

ANA MARIA: Sister, you feel left out 'cause you've never been grilled ... tied to a metal bed and had electricity forced through your body, 'cause you've never been raped by trained dogs, 'cause you've never had mice shoved up your vagina?

CLAUDIA: Did you? – Do they still do that?

CLAUDIA: No, actually I'm just making it up.

BUS DRIVER: (*referring to another curve*) Hang on, girls.

CLAUDIA: I'm sorry, I didn't mean to sound so ... I've just met you and it feels like I've ... but you're a stranger on a bus. Maybe we're soul sisters.

ANA MARIA: Cut the crap.

CLAUDIA: I'm serious! We wouldn't be this connected if we –

ANA MARIA: Weren't forced to sit next to each other for thirty-six hours? I'm going to the bathroom; I think I'm going to be sick.

ANA MARIA leaves.

BUS DRIVER: Even through the blizzard, I can still feel the peace in these mountains. What a beautiful place.

Claudia has a memory.

NANA: (*to FIVE-YEAR-OLD CLAUDIA and her LITTLE SISTER*) Listen to Nana: if they come here, tell them you don't know where Mommy and Daddy are. Remember that Mommy and Daddy can't be found. They're hiding in a safe place. When they ask you where your Mommy and Daddy are, say "I don't know." Do you understand?

Soldiers enter and grab NANA.

NANA: Who do you think you are? You could be my grandson!

SOLDIER #2: (*to girls, brandishing a Hershey's chocolate bar*) Where are they? Where are Mommy and Daddy? Tell me where Mommy and Daddy are and it's all yours ... I'm just going to have to execute you. One, two, three ... FIRE!

FATHER runs in.

FATHER: How dare you pick on children, you sons of whores! Fascist cowards!

The soldiers beat up FATHER.

SCENE THREE

The next day. The passengers are drinking, eating, and chatting. BUS DRIVER has the radio on and cumbia music is playing. MANUEL is at CLAUDIA and ANA MARIA's seat. They're drinking wine.

CLAUDIA: (*holding up a bottle*) Woo! To think I don't have to boycott it here!

MANUEL: Fuck boycotting wine!

BUS DRIVER: We'll be at the border in the next thirty minutes! Have your papers ready!

ANA MARIA: Let's have a toast!

CLAUDIA: To us! To meeting you!

MANUEL: Yeah! To meeting two babes!

DON MARTIN: Only thirty minutes left in bloody Argentina!

DON FERNANDO: Only thirty minutes till we see the Chilean flag!

DON MARTIN and DON FERNANDO: *¡CHI, CHI, CHI! LE, LE, LE! VIVA CHILE!*

ALL: *¡CHI, CHI, CHI! LE, LE, LE! VIVA CHILE!*

MANUEL: Claudia, I want to give you this bracelet. The guy I walked to Argentina with gave it to me at the end of our journey. We met in the mountains, scared shitless, nothing to lose. If it hadn't been for him, I don't think I would have made it. I never saw him again. But I never took this bracelet off.

CLAUDIA: Jesus. Uh … thanks.

MANUEL: Read it.

CLAUDIA: (*reading the inscription on the bracelet*) "We may be fucked, but we're still happy." I don't know what to say.

MANUEL: Just promise me you'll leave it on throughout your journey home.

CLAUDIA: I promise. Hey! Let's get someone to take a picture of us! Hold on a sec!

The music on the radio stops short and ANNOUNCER's voice comes on.

ANNOUNCER: Three alleged terrorists were caught in Valdivia yesterday after a surprise raid on their homes. The three, known to be student leaders at the Andes University, are Teresa Gutiérrez, Isabel Silva, and José Godoy de la Cruz. They were found with large collections of Russian arms and communist propaganda in their homes. The three were taken into the National Centre of Investigations' southern headquarters early yesterday morning. They have confessed to taking part in a plan to assassinate President Augusto Pinochet. An investigation is currently underway throughout Chile.

Cumbia music comes on again.

DON MARTIN: Good for them. I hope they catch them all.

MANUEL: This is scary, man. (*on his feet, holding up a bottle of wine*) And he will fall!

DON FERNANDO, DOÑA MARUJA, CLAUDIA, MANUEL, and ANA MARIA (*definitely not as passionate as the rest*): And he will fall! And he will fall!

MANUEL: (*jumping*) Whoever doesn't jump is Pinochet!

DON FERNANDO, DOÑA MARUJA, CLAUDIA, MANUEL, and ANA MARIA: (*jumping*) Whoever doesn't jump is Pinochet!

DON FERNANDO, DOÑA MARUJA, CLAUDIA, MANUEL, and ANA MARIA repeat this line (while jumping) a few times.

BUS DRIVER: Stop that, you idiots. Do you want us to crash?

MANUEL: (*dancing*) Whoever doesn't dance is Pinochet!

DON FERNANDO, DOÑA MARUJA, CLAUDIA, MANUEL, and ANA MARIA: (*dancing*) Whoever doesn't dance is Pinochet!

Again, DON FERNANDO, DOÑA MARUJA, CLAUDIA, MANUEL, and ANA MARIA repeat this line (while dancing) a few times. ANA MARIA makes her way to the bathroom while the others dance.

BUS DRIVER: (*turning off radio*) Okay! That's enough!

MANUEL: We will not let this get us down! This just goes to show that in Chile, there is resistance!

DON MARTIN: You call a bunch of punks with Russian arms "resistance"? You fuckin' fool!

DOÑA MARUJA: It's the military themselves! They make those stories up to have an excuse to kill our youth!

MANUEL, DON FERNANDO, and CLAUDIA: And he will fall! And he will fall!

DON MARTIN: If the General didn't do this, we'd end up in anarchy!

MANUEL: Let's have a toast to those three brave students!

DON FERNANDO, DOÑA MARUJA, and CLAUDIA: A toast!

DON MARTIN: You drunk commie! (*going to punch MANUEL*)

MANUEL: Fascist pig! Son of a thousand whores!

The other passengers break up the fight before it can start. CLAUDIA starts to slowly make her way to the bathroom.

BUS DRIVER: I said that's enough!

DOÑA MARUJA: I don't know about the rest of you, and may God forgive me for what I'm about to say, but I find it hard to believe our Lord exists at times. I wonder what atrocities they did to those poor children. University students. Educated children. The poor mothers.

MANUEL: It has to end! He will fall this year! They say this, 1986, is the decisive year! We have to make him fall!

BUS DRIVER: Yes, we have to make him fall, but not with terrorism.

MANUEL: But brother, who's the terrorist here, those students or the military?

DOÑA MARUJA: I say the dictatorship!

DON FERNANDO: Don't get so excited, old lady. Our boss here has a point! I don't want Pinochet in power, just like the next guy, but you're right, we can't have our youth resorting to the same means as the military!

DON MARTIN: Now you're talking.

DON FERNANDO: If they kill a few military men, that won't solve the problem; new ones will take their place.

DOÑA MARUJA: I would never hurt a fly, you know that, but I swear that in the days after the coup –

BUS DRIVER: Saving of the Fa –

MANUEL AND DON FERNANDO: Military coup!

DOÑA MARUJA: Thank you. In the days after the coup I witnessed the military do so many horrendous things to our youngsters, that I wish I'd had more than my broom to fight back with.

DON FERNANDO: Yeah! You should have seen my old lady! One day they were beating on a teenager outside our door. We were all lying on the floor, 'cause we could hear shots, and before I knew it she was out in the street, hitting the soldiers with the broom!

DOÑA MARUJA: And I got them to stop beating on the poor saint, too! Angel of God, he was a bloody mess. I offered him some herbs after we'd cleaned him up.

MANUEL: My old lady has an old gun in the house, in case of robbers. But she confessed to me once that she'd gladly blow away one of the uniformed men if she ever got the chance.

DON MARTIN: And then what? What has our country come to when our old ladies turn violent? Huh? Somebody answer me that!

MANUEL: What has our country come to when even a fascist pig like you, who supports the dictator, is in exile? You answer me that!

DON MARTIN: I left of my own free will! All you people who want communism don't realize that if Chile was still communist, you would never have been able to leave in the first place! A barbed-wire wall would have been built around our country, and we'd be stuck inside it!

CLAUDIA has arrived at the bathroom.

SCENE FOUR

In the bathroom. ANA MARIA is holding the envelope and a lighter.

CLAUDIA: Are you okay?

ANA MARIA: Get the fuck out of here.

CLAUDIA: Look at me, I'm shaking.

ANA MARIA: Get the fuck out now 'cause I gotta puke.

CLAUDIA: Why do you keep trying to be so tough? If you need to cry, Ana Maria, just cry. If it was my friend, I think I would have had a nervous break –

ANA MARIA: Look. Just get out. Now. Or I will puke all over you.

CLAUDIA: I just want to help you.

ANA MARIA: Didn't you listen to the fuckin' radio? The pigs are arresting a lot of people now, they've got roadblocks up – José, Teresa, and Isabel know me. They know what I look like.

CLAUDIA: But they'd never tell.

ANA MARIA: Have you ever been tortured? ... I'll probably be busted at the border.

DOÑA MARUJA: (*outside the bathroom*) Girls? Is everything alright in there?

CLAUDIA: Yeah! I'm just feeling a bit sick! Too much Chilean wine after all those years of boycotts!

DOÑA MARUJA: Oh! Well I'll bring you some herbs –

CLAUDIA: No! I'm fine, thanks! I'll be right out.

DOÑA MARUJA: Well I'll prepare you some anyway, for when you come out!

CLAUDIA: Thank you! Why don't you just get off the bus if you're gonna be busted?

ANA MARIA: Don't be an idiot. It's twenty below out there, and we're in the middle of nowhere!

CLAUDIA: I'll get off with you. We can walk, or wait till somebody picks us up –

ANA MARIA: Like the cops?

CLAUDIA: Way up here?

ANA MARIA: What do you think the others would think if we all of a sudden bolted from sight minutes after the news flash – that's like wearing a sign on your back: "I'm in the Resistance."

CLAUDIA: Are you?

ANA MARIA: Don't ever ask anybody that in Chile.

CLAUDIA: You're not anybody. What's in the envelope?

ANA MARIA: I don't know.

CLAUDIA: What do you mean you don't know? Isn't it yours?

ANA MARIA: No. It's not.

CLAUDIA: I can take it across.

ANA MARIA: No.

CLAUDIA: Is it true? Do you guys really have a plan to kill him?

ANA MARIA: No comment.

CLAUDIA: Good. I'm all for it. Jesus, I can't believe I said that, me, Miss Non-Violence –

ANA MARIA: One more tourist remark and I swear I'll –

CLAUDIA: Tell me what to do. I wanna put in my grain of sand.

BUS DRIVER: (*from the driver's seat*) We're at the border!

ANA MARIA: Take the envelope across. Whatever you do, don't open it. If you see yourself in deep shit, burn it. If you get busted, it doesn't matter; if you get busted with this, it does.

CLAUDIA: Okay.

ANA MARIA: Stop shaking. Don't worry. You have a Canadian passport.

CLAUDIA: Where do I take it?

ANA MARIA: Somebody will sit next to you on the bus. (*taking off her scarf and putting it around CLAUDIA's neck*) They'll ask you where you got the scarf; you must answer: "At the Mapuche store in Neuquén." Got it?

CLAUDIA: Got it.

SCENE FIVE

At the border.

LA GRINGA gets on the bus.
Everybody is back in their seats.

BUS DRIVER: This is a strange place to be getting on the bus!

LA GRINGA: Yeah, I was doing some work on the Indian Reserve near here, and now I'm heading back to Valdivia.

BUS DRIVER: Oh! You must be one of those Yankee anthropologists!

LA GRINGA: No, no. I'm Swedish. And I'm a nun. I'm a missionary, actually.

DOÑA MARUJA: (*to DON FERNANDO*) A nun! Who would ever know!

BUS DRIVER: A nun! Well, in that case, please, make yourself comfortable. (*to the passengers*) Did you hear that? A nun! You better behave, all of you! A nun!

LA GRINGA sits down. GARCIA
and CAMPOS get on the bus.

CAMPOS: (*to DOÑA MARUJA*) Where are you going?

DOÑA MARUJA: Río Bueno.

CAMPOS: What for?

DOÑA MARUJA: To visit my children.

GARCIA: How much money have you got?

DOÑA MARUJA: A thousand pesos.

GARCIA: Lady, I'm afraid I can't let you in.

DOÑA MARUJA: Oh dear God. Please, sir, let me in.

CAMPOS: You can live for a couple of days in Chile with a thousand pesos. I can't have people coming in to visit with no money.

DOÑA MARUJA: But I'm Chilean. I've come to visit my children. It's the first time in two years. I'll be staying with them, sir. Please.

CAMPOS: What do you do in Argentina?

DOÑA MARUJA: I'm a maid.

CAMPOS: Why did you leave Chile?

DOÑA MARUJA: To look for work.

CAMPOS: How long do you want to stay here?

DOÑA MARUJA: For two weeks.

GARCIA: That's too long. A thousand pesos will barely buy you bread and butter for a couple of days.

DON FERNANDO: Excuse me, sir. We're Chilean. Please. What is the problem?

CAMPOS: It's not your turn, sir.

DON FERNANDO: I'm her husband.

CAMPOS: How much money have you got?

DON FERNANDO: We've got a thousand pesos between the two of us.

GARCIA: I don't know.

CAMPOS: Let them in, Garcia. They just want to visit their children.

GARCIA: Alright, alright. I hope you realize I'm breaking rules here.

DOÑA MARUJA: You're a saint. Thank you, my dear. God will reward you.

DON FERNANDO: I can't thank you enough.

CAMPOS: Check to make sure these people aren't smuggling anything.

GARCIA: Yes, sir.

CAMPOS, DON FERNANDO and BUS DRIVER get off the bus to retrieve their bag. CAMPOS goes through the bag. As this is happening, GARCIA approaches MANUEL. MANUEL shows GARCIA his ID.

GARCIA: I'm afraid this is fake.

MANUEL: What?

GARCIA: What do you think I am? A fool? This is fake!

MANUEL: I don't know what you're talking about.

GARCIA: Campos! Come back here! Were they smuggling anything?

CAMPOS: (*back on bus*) No, sir.

DON FERNANDO and BUS DRIVER get back on the bus and sit in their respective seats.

GARCIA: Good. Get this man off the bus. His ID card is fake. I'm going to have to question him.

CAMPOS: Yes, sir.

CAMPOS takes MANUEL off. GARCIA follows.

Outside the bus. The following dialogue occurs while GARCIA and CAMPOS manhandle MANUEL in order to conceal from watching passengers and BUS DRIVER that MANUEL is an informer.

GARCIA: How's it going, Pereira?

MANUEL: Great.

GARCIA: It's the old couple, right?

MANUEL: Naw, they're harmless.

CAMPOS: Well, then, which one? The bus driver?

GARCIA: No, no. He's got nothing to do with anything.

GARCIA: Cut the crap and tell us which one. Now.

MANUEL: To tell you the truth, I don't think there's anyone on this bus that –

GARCIA: Listen here, you fuckin' wimp, we know there's a subversive –

CAMPOS: Stop being so nice to the motherfucker. Come on, Pereira. Tell us, or we're going to have to send you back to the rat pit.

MANUEL: There's nothing to tell –

CAMPOS: And this time, we won't just pull out your mother's fingernails.

MANUEL: I think it's the young woman.

CAMPOS: That's more like it. The rich bitch?

MANUEL: No, no. The other one.

CAMPOS: Oh, yeah.

MANUEL: Very careful about what she says and I watched her reaction after the news flash on the three students.

GARCIA: Okay. We'll bust her and take her straight to the National Centre of Investigations. (*to CAMPOS*) Handcuff him, take his bag, and take him away. Make it look rough.

CAMPOS: My pleasure.

CAMPOS takes MANUEL offstage.
GARCIA gets back on the bus.

GARCIA: Let's hope we don't have any more smartasses here today. (*to ANA MARIA*) ID. It says here that your name is Ana Maria Fuentes Mancilla.

ANA MARIA: That's right.

CAMPOS comes back on the bus.

GARCIA: I have reasons to believe otherwise.

ANA MARIA: What?

GARCIA: Unfortunately, you're making my job difficult today. (*to CAMPOS*) Campos, take the lady away.

CAMPOS: Yes, sir.

CAMPOS takes ANA MARIA off. They exit.

GARCIA: (*taking CLAUDIA's passport*) Oh, we've got a Canadian with us today.

CLAUDIA: Yes.

GARCIA: But you were born here. Welcome back to Chile. I hope you have a pleasant stay in this beautiful country of ours. Maybe you'll like it so much you won't want to leave.

CLAUDIA: (*receiving passport back*) Thank you.

GARCIA: (*to BUS DRIVER*) Carry on.

CLAUDIA has a memory.

PLIN PLIN: Hi, boys and girls. Gather round. Do you remember the little girl who was lost? Good! Well, there she was wondering what to do, weeping in the darkness, when she remembered what her mother had said: "If you're ever lost, just let the Southern Cross lead you back home." So she gathered herself and looked up. But the sky was different with other stars ... just the moon and the sun were the same.

SCENE SIX

The bus is moving again.

DOÑA MARUJA: I don't believe that those men are Chileans. How can they do that to their own kind? Two healthy youths, in the best years of their lives, and they take them away! And us! We all just sat around and watched! We're a country of cowards, that's what we are!

DON MARTIN: They had fake IDs! Didn't you hear the gentlemen?

DOÑA MARUJA: Those men aren't gentlemen! Those are a disgrace.

BUS DRIVER: I can't even remember a time when the authorities were here to protect us.

DOÑA MARUJA: How are you feeling, my dear?

CLAUDIA: I guess I'll be okay.

BUS DRIVER: Be careful in Chile. Keep your eyes and ears open.

CLAUDIA: I just can't believe I'm in Chile right now. I mean these mountains, these snowflakes, this road, it's all Chilean!

DOÑA MARUJA: Good for you, my saint. You're looking at the bright side of things. You've been waiting for many years to be on Chilean land, and now here you finally are.

DON FERNANDO: In a few hours, we'll be eating *cazuela* and dancing the *cueca*!

DOÑA MARUJA: (*to LA GRINGA*) Miss Nun, why don't you come sit here next to Claudita, you look so alone over there.

LA GRINGA: Oh, thank you. Sure. Why not? (*doing so*) You don't have to call me Miss Nun, just call me La Gringa, everybody else does.

DOÑA MARUJA: Oh, of course. Are you a Catholic nun, Gringa?

LA GRINGA: Naturally.

DOÑA MARUJA: And Swedish! You speak such good Spanish. How long have you been here?

LA GRINGA: Six years, and before you ask the next question, yes, I like it very much and I feel very much at home here.

DOÑA MARUJA: Isn't that something? Well good for you.

CLAUDIA: What reserve were you on?

LA GRINGA: Oh, one of the Mapuche reserves. I mostly do First Aid and Literacy.

DOÑA MARUJA: (*to DON FERNANDO*) Don't you feel ashamed of yourself? Here she is, Swedish and working for Chileans, while we sit back and complain and do nothing!

DON FERNANDO: Let me sleep, old lady. I'm trying to get some rest before we get to Río Bueno!

DOÑA MARUJA: Good! Sleep off that drunkenness! Claudita, do you think I could put those headphones of yours on? I've been dying to try them.

CLAUDIA: You mean my Walkman? Of course! Here. I'll put on the latest Mercedes Sosa for you, I just got it in Buenos Aires. Here's the volume.

DOÑA MARUJA: Oh, I feel like a modern teenager with these!

DOÑA MARUJA sits back in her seat and listens to the Walkman. DON MARTIN nods off.

LA GRINGA: Where did you get that scarf?

CLAUDIA: At the Mapuche store in Neuquén.

LA GRINGA sits there with an expectant look on her face.

LA GRINGA: Do you have the envelope?

CLAUDIA: Yes.

LA GRINGA: Good. Now's the perfect time to give it to me.

CLAUDIA: Right. So I just hand it to you and that's it.

LA GRINGA: Yes.

CLAUDIA hands her the envelope.

LA GRINGA: First time?

CLAUDIA: Yeah. I'm sorry.

LA GRINGA: It's okay.

CLAUDIA: For me this is a one-shot deal. She asked me to do this 'cause she knew she was gonna get busted.

LA GRINGA: Who?

CLAUDIA: The woman who was arrested at –

LA GRINGA: Hold on, you mean that isn't your scarf?

CLAUDIA: She thinks they found out about her through the three students that were caught in Valdivia –

LA GRINGA: Okay, I've got to figure out a way to get off this bus. (*to BUS DRIVER*) Are you going to be stopping soon?

BUS DRIVER: Well, the next stop is Río Bueno, so the old couple can get off.

LA GRINGA: I see. Thank you.

BUS DRIVER: Wait a minute. What's going on up there? Son of a bitch, they already have a roadblock up way out here, all because of the Student Union kids and their crazy ideas –

LA GRINGA hands the envelope back to CLAUDIA.

LA GRINGA: Take it to the bathroom and burn it. Fast.

CLAUDIA goes to the bathroom. The other passengers start to wake up. The bus comes to a stop. Two SECRET POLICE agents come on the bus.

SECRET POLICE #1: (*to LA GRINGA*) You. Get off the bus. (*to SECRET POLICE #2*) Stay here and keep an eye on everybody.

SECRET POLICE #2: Yes, sir.

SECRET POLICE #1 and LA GRINGA get off the bus. He takes her offstage. The sound of gunshots. DOÑA MARUJA wails. SECRET POLICE #1 comes back, gun pulled.

SECRET POLICE #1: (*to BUS DRIVER*) Are these all the people you have on the bus?! Is this it?!

BUS DRIVER: No, sir. There's a girl in the bathroom. I'm sure she's just sick, sir.

SECRET POLICE #1: (*to SECRET POLICE #2*) Go check the bathroom!

SECRET POLICE #2: Yes, sir.

In the bathroom. CLAUDIA has the lighter in her hand, and is reading the contents of the envelope.

CLAUDIA: "My dearest Juan, it is a long night in July, dimly lit by a pale, pale Patagonian moon. The wind howls through the deserted streets and rocks my empty bed, as I remember our summer in Vina" – What the fuck?!

SECRET POLICE #2 enters the bathroom, gun pulled.

SECRET POLICE #2: Hurry up! Use your lighter! (*sticking his head out of the bathroom, to SECRET POLICE #1*) She's throwing up all over the place!

Back in the bathroom, he sees CLAUDIA starting to burn the paper. He grabs it from her, puts it out, takes the lighter, and holds it up to the paper. Secret writing shows up.

SECRET POLICE #2: Don't burn it! Look! "Meet at the Haiti Café in Santiago on the 31st at 5:00 p.m. ... Contact will be wearing a red dress ... Drive to allotted house and retrieve arms ... Assassination of Pinochet is final. The fox will finally die." Do as it tells you.

He lights the paper and lets it burn, stomping on it on the bathroom floor. CLAUDIA begins to vomit.

CLAUDIA: It's okay. I'm alright. I'll do it.

Gun still drawn, he pulls CLAUDIA out of the bathroom.

SECRET POLICE #2: (*to SECRET POLICE #1*) She wouldn't stop.

SECRET POLICE #1: Okay, fine. Let her sit down. (*to BUS DRIVER*) Continue on your way. (*to SECRET POLICE #2*) Let's go.

SECRET POLICE #1 and *SECRET POLICE #2 get off the bus.*

SCENE SEVEN

DOÑA MARUJA and DON FERNANDO are grooming themselves.

DOÑA MARUJA: (*wiping DON FERNANDO's shoulders*) Just look at that dandruff! Dear God!

DON FERNANDO: It's dust, woman!

DOÑA MARUJA: (*to CLAUDIA*) Well, my special girl, you take good care of yourself. Keep wearing that bracelet that Manuel gave you and pray to the Virgin to watch over you. (*handing her a crumpled piece of paper*) Here's our address in Río Bueno. Come stay with us before you go.

CLAUDIA: You've been very kind to me; thank you for everything. If there's anything I can do for you –

DOÑA MARUJA: There is: don't forget us.

CLAUDIA: Never. (*handing her the Walkman*) Doña Maruja, this is for you.

DOÑA MARUJA: Thank you, my dear Claudita. I will always cherish it.

BUS DRIVER: Okay! Here we are in Río Bueno!

DOÑA MARUJA: Bye, my dear! And don't forget what I told you!

CLAUDIA: I won't! Bye!

DON FERNANDO and DOÑA MARUJA embrace CLAUDIA. They get off the bus.

DON FERNANDO: *Chilecito,* here I come!

The BUS DRIVER hands them their bag and they walk offstage, waving back to DON MARTIN and CLAUDIA. BUS DRIVER gets back on the bus and the bus leaves again.

BUS DRIVER: Almost there. Fresh fish. Mmm.

DON MARTIN: (*handing CLAUDIA a handkerchief*) Don't cry. You'll meet many more beautiful people in Chile.

CLAUDIA: Thank you.

DON MARTIN: I have to admit this has been a hard trip, but you'll soon see for yourself that Chile has never been better. How long are you going to stay?

CLAUDIA: I don't know. I'll travel around a bit. What about you? What are you going to do?

DON MARTIN: I'm going to grow roots here again.

CLAUDIA: Do you have family here?

DON MARTIN: Some kids and grandkids.

CLAUDIA: No wife?

DON MARTIN: No. She died. In Argentina. Caught pneumonia one winter and never recovered. Good old Meche. Good woman. But hey, look at this beautiful country of ours! We're down from the mountains! No more blizzard! Heck, it's so green down here

I can smell the sweet grass! Look at those flowers, covered in dew – did you know that my oldest grandson, Panchito, would ask me, "Grandpa, why do the flowers cry in the morning?" So I'd say, "They're not crying, Panchito, it's dew," but the little bugger would insist: "Look! The sun's making their tears shine!" I'd just answer that the sun was drying up their tears, and you know what the hard-headed rascal would say?

CLAUDIA: What?

DON MARTIN: "The sun is drying their tears, but tomorrow they'll wake up crying again."

CLAUDIA: Wow.

DON MARTIN: I said, "Yes, but let's just live for today."

BUS DRIVER: Goddammit, we finally made it! Here we are! Valdivia!

"Vuelvo para vivir" by Illapu starts to play.

CLAUDIA: Is this it? (*looking around*) Oh my God!

Stage slowly fades to black.

The whole song must be played
through bows and walkout.

The End.

CHILE CON CARNE

PRODUCTION HISTORY

Chile Con Carne was first produced at Station Street Arts Centre in Vancouver from October 12 to 21, 1995, by Norte-Sur Arts Association of the Americas, with the following cast and crew:

MANUELITA	Carmen Aguirre
MOTHER'S VOICE	Ana Duran
FATHER'S VOICE	Patricio Ibarra
PELAO'S VOICE	Carlos Reygadas
FLACA'S VOICE	Carmen Rodríguez

Director and Dramaturge	Guillermo Verdecchia
Set and Costume Designer	Cecilia Boisier
Sound Designer	Alejandro Verdecchia
Lighting Designer	Michael Hirano
Production and Stage Manager	Michel Bisson
Promotion Photographer	Alejandra Aguirre
Slide Designer	Tim Matheson
Painters (for poster and slides)	Cecilia Boisier and Nora Patrich
Publicist	Helen Nestor

Chile Con Carne was made possible thanks to financial assistance from the Canada Council for the Arts and the British Columbia Arts Council.

CHARACTERS

MANUELITA, age eight
MOTHER'S VOICE
FATHER'S VOICE
PELAO'S VOICE
FLACA'S VOICE

SETTING

Vancouver, the mid-1970s.

PROLOGUE

Seventies disco music has been playing through the walk-in. The stage is in darkness. There is a tree upstage right, a big trunk downstage right, and a child's school desk downstage left. There is a screen or sheet suspended on the back wall of the stage. The whole set – except for the tree – is painted like the sky, with hints of clouds.

At various points in the play, slides are projected onto the screen at the back of the stage. Some slides contain words, others just an image.

"Venceremos" by Inti-Illimani plays – or any other Inti-Illimani song celebrating Salvador Allende's rise to power. One verse of this celebratory song plays, accompanied by a number of slides showing Salvador Allende and popular rallies in Chile during Allende's term. These slides are projected onto the screen at the back of the stage. The verse is brutally interrupted by the sound of a huge bomb. The bomb sound effect coincides with slides of the Presidential Palace in Santiago being bombed on September 11, 1973.

From the bomb we go right into a small fragment of Allende's final speech, hours before his death, in which Allende talks about the great avenues being open once again in the future, where Chileans will walk freely. He then says, "Long live Chile! Long live the people! Long live the workers! These are my last words" – Allende's most famous words. Throughout this section slides of Allende resisting at the Presidential Palace, with his helmet and rifle, surrounded by members of his government, are projected.

SLIDE: "Mom, Dad, and Friends
Discuss Tactics in the Living Room."

Four adult voices – two men and two women – are heard talking very animatedly and loudly in Chilean Spanish. (Note: It is very important that the actors chosen to record the voices be Chilean, in order to capture the accent and intonation. There should be no pauses in the adults' discussion; they are continually interrupting one another.)

Moments after the discussion starts, English subtitles appear on slides at the back of the stage. Mixed in with the subtitles is also a slide of an empanada and some wine.

FATHER: *No, po compadres, la cuestión es, compadres, que los compañeros en Chile sepan que nosotros estamos súper comprometidos con la causa, po, compadres –*

SLIDE: "We want our comrades in Chile to know that we are very committed to the cause."

PELAO: *Claro, po huevón, por eso mismo yo propongo que hagamos una buena peña, po huevón, completa con empanadas y unas buenas cumbias.*

SLIDE: "Yeah. We should have a big benefit party with lots of empanadas and good music."

MOTHER: *Yo estoy de acuerdo con el Pelao, ah, porque pucha que a los gringos les gusta bailar salsa y a lo mejor un puro baile de salsa va a ser suficiente –*

SLIDE: "Yeah. Gringos love to dance salsa and maybe a good salsa session will be enough."

FLACA: *Chucha, con que vengan los puros chilenos llenamos el Russian Hall, y más con los gringos, pooo. A que llegan quinientas personas, y de paso hueveamos un rato y la pasamos bien, po –*

> *SLIDE: "Yeah. The Chileans can fill up the Russian Hall even without the gringos, so imagine with them. I bet we will attract at least five hundred people and we'll have a good time."*

FATHER: *Pero ustedes conchas de su madre, chucha pareciera que solo quieren revolverlas nomás, po. Pero hay que comprobarles a los presos en Chile que nosotros apoyamos su huelga de hambre –*

> *SLIDE: "But you guys! It would seem that we just wanna have fun. We need to prove to the prisoners in Chile that we support their hunger strike."*

MOTHER: *Pero no seais huevón. Yo no pienso hacer ninguna huelga de hambre –*

> *SLIDE: "Don't be a dick. I'm not gonna do a hunger strike."*

FLACA: *Yo tampoco, ah, mira que ya estoy más flaca que la cresta, ah –*

> *SLIDE: "Me neither. I'm skinny enough as it is."*

FATHER: *¿Y como creis que están los compañeros en Chile, que en la cárcel no les dan ni agua, po, compañera?*

> *SLIDE: "But how do you think our comrades in Chile are? They don't even give them water in jail."*

MOTHER: *Oye, corta el hueveo. Lo que necesitamos hacer es juntar plata pa' mandarles a las mujeres de los presos pa'a que puedan alimentar a los cabros chicos. La mejor manera es tener un baile de salsa y vender hartos tragos pa'a que los gringos tomen –*

SLIDE: "That's enough. What we need is to raise money for the prisoners' wives, so they can feed their kids. The best way is to have a big dance and sell lots of booze to the gringos."

PELAO: *Y hartas empanadas, po comadre.*

SLIDE: "And a lot of empanadas, too."

MOTHER: *Ya, po, hartas empanadas pa'a que los gringos coman harto también. No vamos a ganar na' de plata haciendo una huelga de hambre acá en Canadá, po huevón. Además, chi, ¿qué te creis? ¿Quién va a cuidar a los cabros nuestros mientras nosotros nos matamos de hambre, concha su madre?*

SLIDE: "Alright, a lot of empanadas so the gringos can also eat a lot. We won't make any money doing a hunger strike. Besides, who do you think will take care of our kids while we starve?"

FATHER: *Oye, si podemos ganar plata, po huevona. Una huelga de hambre causaría sensación acá en Canadá. Tú que tanto te preocupáis por los gringos, ya po, ¿tu creis que los gringos no van a donar plata cuando vean un montón de chilenos en la United Church haciendo una huelga de hambre en solidaridad con los compañeros en Chile? ¡Si a los gringos se les cae la baba por huevadas así! Van a llegar la tele, los diarios, las radios, y los compadres en Chile van a saber que no nos estamos puro rascando las hue'as – Además, la plata que se done se manda directo a las familias de los presos –*

SLIDE: "Yes, we will. A hunger strike will be a sensation here. Since you care for the gringos: I'm sure they will donate money when they see a big group of Chileans doing a hunger strike at the United Church in solidarity with our comrades in Chile. Gringos love shit like that. We will attract the TV, the newspapers, the radio… Then the comrades in Chile will know we're not just sitting around scratching our balls. Besides, we'll send all the money we raise directly to the families of political prisoners."

PELAO: *Oiga compadre, entiendo su propuesta pero la comadre tiene razón, po. ¿Qué hacemos con nuestros cabros chicos?*

SLIDE: "Listen buddy, I understand your motion but our friend here is right. What do we do with our kids?"

FLACA: *Chucha, que me están aburriendo hasta las hueva'as, ¿por qué no hacemos las dos cuestiones no más? Baile de salsa y huelga de hambre. Y a propósito, hay una galla que es súper buena artista y que se ofreció pa'a hacer los posters de "Boycott Chilean Goods" –*

SLIDE: "Shit, I'm getting bored with all this. Why don't we just do both? Why don't we have a salsa dance and a hunger strike? By the way, I know a woman who is a very good artist and offered to create the 'Boycott Chilean Goods' posters."

PLAY

When MOTHER is saying, "Don't be a dick," MANUELITA comes running in and the lights go up. She listens to her parents, decides that their conversation is boring, and goes directly to the trunk. She opens it and it spills over with "dress-up": old slips and nightgowns and a few old, matted blonde wigs of different lengths.

MANUELITA is wearing her hair in two braids that stick out of the side of her head – not straight out like Pippi Longstocking, just out – with a part in the middle. She wears bell-bottomed barf-coloured corduroy pants that are too short, black patent leather shoes with frilly pink socks, and a red polyester T-shirt that says "Disneyland" on it. She carries a packet of Tang.

MANUELITA checks out the dress-ups and finally decides to wear only a blonde wig for today. She listens to her parents again, decides that they're still boring, and leaves the house. MANUELITA should leave as FLACA finishes saying "Boycott Chilean Goods." The voices cut out abruptly. MANUELITA climbs her tree and starts eating her Tang straight out of the package.

SLIDE: A child's drawing of a tree.

MANUELITA eats her Tang and watches the passersby. She looks out into the audience and realizes she is being watched. She offers the audience some Tang.

MANUELITA: This is Cedar. I found him a year ago. The day after we got here. There's no trees like Cedar in Valparaíso. There's all these tractors here and gringos too. They're all down there. They're chopping all the trees down. I think they wanna make a house here. I don't care what they do to the other trees. As long as they don't chop Cedar down.

I come here every day after school to have my snacks and watch the passersby. This is where I read the letters from my grandma and Gabriela. Nobody knows about Cedar. Not even Joselito. He's like my cousin.

MANUELITA climbs down the tree and goes to the desk.

SLIDE: A can of chili con carne.

"O Canada" plays. MANUELITA hangs on to her crotch, desperate to pee. When the anthem is over, she sits at her desk.

(*to the audience*) Everyone at school thinks I'm mute. So they always say things to me, 'cause they know I'm not gonna talk back. "Fuck you, bitch," and "Hey, Speedy Gonzalez, why don't you speedy back home," and "You're from Chile, chili con carne."

So today is just another mute day for me. Same as always. Miss Mitten goes from desk to desk helping kids out with their reading and I'm sitting really still, with my legs crossed like a señorita, 'cause I really have to go pee but I don't know how to say it, when all of a sudden somebody brings their desk over and sits beside me!

It's the beautiful honey-coloured girl! Honey eyes, honey freckles, honey skin, honey hair. She's wearing French-cut jeans and her lunch kit has Charlie's Angels on it! She's smiling at me with her really shiny braces, and she even has a watch! And little pearl earrings!

"Rrrr Leslie. Rrr?"

"Lassie"

"*Leslie*"

"Lassie."

"*Leslie.* L-E-S-L-I-E."

SLIDE: Lassie the dog.

Her name is Lassie! I remember in Chile I used to watch *Lassie* on TV. I didn't know any dogs like Lassie in Chile. All the dogs I used to know had scabies and ran around the neighbourhood in packs.

My friend Lassie is talking and talking still and pointing at the door. She looks at my crotch. We look at my crotch. She wants to take me to the bathroom 'cause I peed my pants.

SLIDE: Two little girls playing on a dirt road in Chile.

MANUELITA faints. The "Faint Song" plays throughout the next section. This is an original composition by the sound designer.

The floor opens up and sucks me in and back, back to the kitchen in Valparaíso where I would help my grandmother make the empanadas, back to the lane where me and Gabriela would swap necklaces made of watermelon seeds, back to the plaza where we got our picture taken with the white donkey full of decorations – I wonder if that picture's still sitting on my grandmother's piano?

MANUELITA sings.

Cabillito blanco llévame de aquí, llévame a mi pueblo donde yo nací, tengo tengo tengo tu no tienes nada ...

MANUELITA gets up from the floor.

SLIDE: Colonia Inglesa bottle.

Me and Lassie are punished. Miss Mitten said we have to stay after school 'cause we were bad. So we're cleaning the cloakroom 'cause Miss Mitten told us to, when I see my dad poke his head in! I run up to him and he picks me up and twirls me around and hugs and kisses me, "*Mi niña Linda, mi reina preciosa, qué pasó, se volvió a mear la niñita, pero mijita, es cuestión de pedir permiso pa'a ir al baño, no más, pucha, si no va a vivir meada la pobre, y se paspa ...*" My dad smells like Colonia Inglesa, he smells like my grandfather and my uncles and all the men in Chile, and that smell, that smell is sad, so sad, but I don't know why.

I remember Lassie, she must think I'm a baby. I tell my dad to put me down right away. I tell him this is my new friend, Lassie. My dad laughs and goes to give her a hug and a kiss, but she takes some steps back and shakes her head. My dad still doesn't understand that gringos don't really touch that much. I'm about to tell him that, when I see Lassie's mother come in!

She's really tall and skinny with long blonde hair and sunglasses. She's wearing high-heeled clogs and bell-bottomed jeans with a white shirt. She's got really long red nails with diamond rings! She's smoking a cigarette.

My dad says, "Jorge González." She says her name and doesn't even shake my dad's hand, she just blows smoke in his face and won't even take off her glasses. She says something to Lassie and starts to leave. Lassie is gathering her stuff and leaving too. She says something to me and waves goodbye.

Me and my dad are outside. We're pushing the car and some boys from grade seven are helping. We always have to push our car. It's really big and smells like a basement. My dad found it, and him and his friends fixed it a bit.

Lassie and her mom are sitting in their car. It's a big pink convertible and it's shiny and new! Her mom is still smoking and bobbing her head up and down, and Lassie's talking and talking.

Finally Lassie comes running out of her car, right to me! She takes my arm and pulls me to her car and she talks and talks. She's really excited! My dad says, "I think she wants you to go visit her!" Wow! Lassie's house! Wow! I've never been to anybody's house here, only to the Chileans', and those don't count. I wonder if her house will be just like the ones on TV! Maybe her house will be like the ones my mother cleans! She says people here have so much money, they throw food in the garbage, and clothes and fridges and furniture – that's where we get our stuff, my mom brings it from the big houses.

My dad has walked up to Lassie's car and he's waving his arms and acting things out for Lassie's mom. He only speaks Spanish, so he has to wave his arms a lot. Lassie's mom just nods and smokes.

My dad says that it's okay. I can go visit Lassie and he'll pick me up before dinner. He got directions and everything. He gives me a hug and a kiss and Lassie takes me to her car. I get in the back seat.

SLIDE: "Manuelita Discovers America."

Rod Stewart's "Da Ya Think I'm Sexy" begins to play.

Lassie's mom is playing the music really loud! She screeches off. She drives just like Charlie's Angels! I look back and see my dad, with all the boys, still pushing the car. He looks up and waves. I watch him get farther and farther away. Before I know it, we're in a neighbourhood I've never seen before. The houses look like the wedding cakes at the store we clean at night, and the sidewalks are so clean even my grandmother would be impressed. I smile and bob my head up and down to the music, just like Lassie's mom. This is my first North American experience. And I am alone.

"This is María," says Lassie. She's a lady that looks like my mother. She's wearing a black dress and an apron. She speaks to me in Spanish. She sounds different. María says she's from Mexico. She says that Lassie told her about me, so Lassie brought me here to meet her. María asks me what part of Mexico I'm from. I say I'm not from Mexico. I'm from Chile. María laughs and says that

Lassie thought I was from Mexico. My throat's got a big knot in it. María's really nice. But I hate her. I wish she would die.

María put my pants and undies in the washer. I'm wearing one of Lassie's pants for now. Lassie's mother has disappeared and me and Lassie are having pink milk and cookies. Just like on TV. Lassie's talking and talking to me and María's polishing silver in the living room. The knot in my throat is getting smaller, so I can swallow my pink milk easy.

Lassie keeps talking and she gets up. I follow her. We go up these big huge stairs and she takes me to a door. She opens it and I see the most beautiful sight in the whole wide world! Lassie's room is full of big white shelves and shelves and shelves of dolls! Some are dolls with soothers and pink dresses! Some come with little baby carriages! They're the most beautiful dolls in the world! Then, I see them! A huge shelf full of Barbies! Barbies! The Barbies have cars and houses and jeeps and swimming pools and all these shoes and clothes and purses and mini-lipsticks and necklaces! I run from shelf to shelf, "*¡Mira ésta! ¡Y ésta! ¡Qué linda! ¿Me puedes regular una, Lassie? ¡Juguemos con ésta! ¡No! ¡Con ésta! ¡Con las dos! ¡Mira! ¡Mira! Te pasaste, Lassie, te pasaste!*"

Lassie's laughing. I'm speaking Spanish and she doesn't understand me.

I hear my dad's voice downstairs. He's talking really loud, like he always does. He's talking in Spanish with María. Lassie says something and laughs, then she says "*Arriba, arriba, ándale, ándale.*" She points at me and laughs. I just laugh too.

MANUELITA lies on her back. It is an echo of when she faints.

SLIDE: Cecilia Boisier's painting of women running with suitcases. Throughout this section we will see numerous slides of Boisier's paintings of people fleeing.

We hear sounds of a military raid on a house with "Misa Criolla" by Ariel Ramírez playing underneath.

Sometimes at night my dad screams in his sleep. He yells out, "No, no!" and my mom has to shake him awake. My mom told me he has dreams at night that the military's going to get him. I remember in Valparaíso when I came from school and they were in the house, checking everything. They were even in the closets.

So now I always check the bathtub before I go pee, just in case there's a military still in there. Even though my mom explained that they're not in Canada. That day, they took my dad away and my mom and grandma were crying. My dad didn't come back.

A whole year later, me, my mom, and my grandma went to Santiago in El Italiano's taxi. My mom and grandma cried the whole time and our suitcases were on the roof. I was wearing the pink dress that Auntie Cuqui made for me and my grandma had curled my hair. We got to the airport and I looked for my dad everywhere 'cause my mom said he'd be there waiting for us. But I didn't see him. Finally we got on the big plane and we saw my dad. He looked different. He was really skinny. My mom climbed on him in front of everybody and my dad hugged her with his one arm. The other hand was handcuffed to the airplane seat. But that was already a long time ago. Almost a year. But my dad still has bad dreams.

MANUELITA goes to Cedar and climbs it.

I went to Lassie's house again. María made us these really funny Canadian sandwiches and Lassie taught me how to say them: "peanut butter and banana."

The tractor people are down there. They're eating and burping like gringos do. There's some fancy gringos all gathered around a thing like a map. They keep pointing right at Cedar.

"Trabajadores al poder" by ¡Karaxú! begins to play. MANUELITA hears it, climbs down from her tree, and goes to her trunk. She puts on a pink nightgown.

SLIDE: A poster that reads "An active resistance demands an active solidarity."

Trabajadores trampolé, trabajadores trampolé ... We're gonna go to a *peña* tonight. That's like a benefit party. My mom and dad and their friends planned everything. We're going to the Ukrainian Hall in Chinatown. My mom said I could dress up, even though it's snowing outside.

A cueca *by Victor Jara begins to play and MANUELITA crosses over to her desk. She sits on top of it.*

We had to pick up Juan of the Chickens on the way here. We call him that because he works at a chicken restaurant. He has to wear a chicken costume. He has to be outside the restaurant and run around, pretending to be a chicken. Sometimes we go visit him and I can see his eyes through the beak. Today he was being a chicken outside the restaurant, but he still doesn't realize it gets slippery when it snows, so he slipped and fell. He twisted his ankle. So that's why we went to pick him up.

"La colegiala" by Rodolfo y su Típica begins to play. MANUELITA gets up.

¡Oye! ¡Juan! ¡Baila conmigo! ¡Ya po!

MANUELITA dances with JUAN.

Now Juan of the Chickens is drinking some wine even though he's not allowed to here 'cause he's only seventeen, and he's saying it's too bad we have to boycott the Chilean kind 'cause this one tastes like shit. Juan of the Chickens arrived just a few months ago. He ran away from the jail in Valparaíso and snuck on a ship. Then they made him get off in Squamish 'cause they found him. He was really skinny and full of burns and bruises. So my mom and dad and their friends had to help him. He was taking care of me once 'cause my mom and dad were busy and he showed me a picture of his girlfriend in Valparaíso. "La Chueca" he calls her, 'cause her legs go like this. He says he's gonna bring her here and I can teach her English. Juan of the Chickens is real excited about La Chueca coming here. He tells me how he writes long letters to her, describing the apartments here, with carpets and fridges and electric stoves and central heating. He tells me this with his eyes wide open, like this.

"Puta, pu, Manuelita. Si vivimos como reyes acá y quiero que la Chueca lo vea, pu."

He never thought he'd be in a country where all you have to do to furnish your house is go through the alleys, and you can even find cars and just fix them. He says he found a white leather couch already and fixed it up, for when La Chueca comes. Juan of the Chickens keeps talking and finally he stops.

"Manuelita, why are you looking at me like that?"

"'Cause I thought you were gonna go back to Chile, with everybody else."

"What are you talking about, little one? No one's going back to Chile for a long, long time."

"Yes, they are! We are! My mom and dad always say we're going back really soon! As soon as he falls!"

SLIDE: Pinochet.

"No, Manuelita. Your mom and dad are on the blacklist, and they're not allowed back in. And he won't fall for a long, long time."

My stomach hurts, like he's hit me in the tummy. I can't breathe. I can't talk. He's a liar, he's a liar, he's a fucking liar. My mom always says we never get any furniture 'cause we're leaving next month, as soon as he falls, she always says, the revolution will come and he will fall, he will fall, that's why we have to work hard, to make him fall, that's why you can't forget, Manuelita, don't ever forget, you are one hundred percent Chilean, Manuelita. You are a mix of Basque blood and Mapuche blood. Don't forget. Don't speak that ugly language, Manuelita, speak Spanish, speak Spanish, you are not Canadian, so don't even try it, speak your language, Manuelita, now!! I run away to the bathroom.

SLIDE: A porcelain doll with the head torn off.

MANUELITA runs to centre stage
and lands on the floor, face down.

I remember my toys sitting on the dresser in Chile, waiting. The porcelain doll passed all the way down from my great-grandmother. The clown with the drum. The table and chairs my father made for me.

My mom comes into the bathroom. She tries to hug me, but I won't let her. I want to say, "Hey, Speedy Gonzalez, why don't you speedy back home," but all I can do is kick.

MANUELITA gets up from the floor.

¡Quiero a mi abuelita! I want my grandma! I see my mother leaning against the wall. I see her hands, swollen from washing too many dishes, one over her mouth, the other against the wall. She's got two bandages, she cut herself making the five hundred empanadas for the *peña*. She lets herself slide down the wall, and rocks back and forth, "*Ay, Dios mío, ayúdame, Dios mío, por favor,*" she says it over and over again. I hear her do this sometimes, but she's never done it in front of me, until now.

"What's the blacklist?"

MANUELITA gets herself up from the
floor and starts to wash her face.

"What's the blacklist?"

"It means your passport is marked."

MANUELITA walks over to the desk and sits on top of it.

We drive home from the *peña*. It's four in the morning, and the streets are deserted.

SLIDE: A Chinese store sign.

It's snowing in Chinatown and the heater in the car doesn't work, my dad has to keep slowing down to wipe the foggy window. My mom is silent.

SLIDE: A neon Chinese restaurant sign.

I see a Chinese sign. "You wanna hear the song Lassie taught me today? ... *Chinese, Japanese, dirty knees, look at these, money please.*"

MANUELITA slaps her face.

"*Cállate, cabra 'e mierda*. Don't you ever say that again. Don't you dare. We're just like them, Manuela del Carmen González Mancilla. We're just like them. We're not like the gringos here, we're like other immigrants. Don't you dare turn against your own kind."

My father's trying to explain, "That's racist, Manuelita. Very racist. Someday you'll understand."

My parents are going on and on about how I'm turning into a gringa already, that we have to go back as soon as possible, that I'm forgetting who I am, this business about wearing the wigs has gone too far, that I want to be a gringa.

How can I tell them that I do? That I would do anything to be a gringa, to have long blonde hair and sparkling blue eyes, to be called Sherry or Sandy, to have David MacWilliams who's in grade four pay attention to me at least once, to be called pretty rather than spic or weirdo or bitch? I would do anything to have my parents and all their friends understand me … I would do anything for a Barbie.

"Since we're on the blacklist and all my dolls are in Chile, can I get a Barbie?"

"Who told you we're on the blacklist?"

"Juan of the Chickens told her. He said he was sorry, he didn't know she didn't know."

"Don't worry, Manuelita. We won't be on the blacklist for long. We're gonna go on a hunger strike till they take us off."

"You idiot. You weren't supposed to tell her yet. Now she's gonna keep pissing her pants in school. Manuelita, we are going to go on a hunger strike, but not for a while. You can see us every day, and then we'll be off the blacklist and we can go back, Grandma says it's not so bad any more in Chile –"

"*I just wanna know if I can get a Barbie!!*"

"Okay, Manuelita, okay. We'll get you a doll."

"*A Barbie!!*"

"A Barbie."

The memory of the setting sun over Valparaíso fades in the neon signs that flash as we drive through the snow.

> *"My Sharona" by the Knack begins to play. MANUELITA goes to her trunk, gets rid of the pink nightgown and dances in front of her mirror, practicing being "Canadian."*

Gawd, you guys. Gawd. Gross. You think you're so great. You guys! You punker. You punker. Show-off, show-off, nuthin' but a show-off.

MANUELITA pulls at her T-shirt, imagining she has breasts. She checks out her ass.

Hi, David.

She runs to Cedar and climbs it.

SLIDE: A tree being chopped down.

I know Cedar's next. He's the only one left standing. I finally decided to tell Joselito about Cedar and the critical situation.

MANUELITA starts tying a bandana around her face.

Joselito said the only way to proceed was armed struggle since you can't have a dialogue with the enemy. Juan of the Chickens was an urban guerilla in Valparaíso so we got some pointers from him.

Tonight's the night. Joselito slept over and we're gonna break the windows on the tractors.

MANUELITA takes out a huge kitchen knife and holds it up to her left index finger.

But first we become blood brothers.

The stage goes black. We hear windows breaking. As the lights come up, we hear the sound of birds chirping. MANUELITA is reading out a letter she has written. Her left index finger has a huge white bandage on it.

SLIDE: A child's letter with a drawing of a snowman and a sled.

The "Letter Song," an original composition by the sound designer, plays softly underneath the letter.

Querida Abuelita,

Estoy aprendiendo a bailar la cueca and disco too. At lunch I go to disco-dancing classes, Grandma, I wish you were here or I was there so I could show you my steps.

Here everything's okay. Papi works really hard at a paper kind of factory, he even has to work all night sometimes, and me and my mom clean a bakery and a hair salon at night. Mami cleans rich people's houses during the day. She brings home nice clothes that they give her.

We have a lot of friends from Chile, Grandma. There's Flaca, who used to be a psychologist and now she works at a hotel, and there's Guatón, who used to be a journalist and now he has two paper routes and he works sometimes at a wiener factory, and lots of others.

At school I made a good friend called Lassie. Just like the dog, she's very nice and very pretty, maybe you can meet her sometime. I'm sending you a drawing of *El Parque de Estanli*: Stanley Park. That's me in the middle. I'm on a sled.

Send many hugs and kisses to everybody in the neighbourhood, especially Gabriela. I love you, *Abuelita.*

Manuelita

MANUELITA puts the letter in an envelope and takes it with her as she slowly walks toward the desk. Music resembling the sound of a heartbeat, composed by the sound designer, plays.

SLIDE: The southern cone of South America.

At school nobody knows I dance *cueca*. Nobody knows I work at the bakery and at the hair salon. Nobody knows my house is always full of my parents' friends having meetings till really late. Nobody knows we have protests and rallies, nobody knows we have *peñas* and salsa dances, nobody knows my parents are going on a hunger strike. Nobody knows my dad was in jail. Nobody knows we're on the blacklist. Nobody from school, not even Lassie, comes over to my house. Nobody knows we have posters of Fidel

Castro and Che Guevara on the walls. Nobody knows about the Chilean me at school.

MANUELITA arrives at the desk.

SLIDE: A Mountie smiling down at a blond boy.

The man from the RCMP is here to talk about safety. So stupid!

MANUELITA sits down at the desk.

He's a huge gringo policeman, with a gun at his side! I bet he knows that me and Joselito broke the windows on the tractors and now he's come to get me. Then I'll be in jail. Just like my dad was. He's standing at the front of the class with a nice warm smile on his face. "Hi, kids," he says. I remember those nice grins, those are the same grins they wore when they raided our house and they tore my favourite doll's head off. I sit in the first row of desks so I can see the gun real clearly. It's real all right, but it's smaller than the ones in Chile. The man starts talking about dangerous men in the woods and never get in cars and never take money from strangers, but I'm thinking, I know. I know what you're really about. My mom explained to me once that the gringos helped to do the coup in Chile, that's why we always have protests outside the U.S. consulate, so I know what you're up to, mister. You're trying to get us to trust you, but "no, sir." He takes his gun out slowly and holds it like this, flat in his hands, he's talking about how he never uses it, when all of a sudden I hear a kid screaming real loud. A few moments go by before I realize it's me that's screaming.

MANUELITA stands on the desk and does a silent scream, turning in a circle. She does a full circle and climbs down, staring down at the seat.

There's a puddle of pee on my seat. Miss Mitten comes up to me with a frozen smile and eyes that are about to pop out. She hits me on the head with her flashcards.

MANUELITA runs to Cedar.

I can hear the kids laughing 'cause I peed, but I run all the way home and here, to Cedar.

MANUELITA climbs up Cedar.

Juan of the Chickens explained that to be an urban guerilla you must use different tactics for your strategy. It's not all just molotov cocktails and burning tires for barricades.

MANUELITA takes the petition that's hanging on a nail from the tree.

So me and Joselito started this petition. We used my dad's Spanish–English dictionary to write it, then Bill, our friend from the refugee hotel, corrected it. Bill's a gringo, and he's the leader of the gringos' solidarity group and Flaca is in love with him. I can tell by the way she looks at him when she puffs on her cigarette. But Flaca can't do anything with Bill 'cause she's married to Pelao. But I saw Bill and Flaca in the backyard once. Me and Joselito were spying on them. Shame, shame, double shame, now I know your boyfriend's name.

I've already got a whole page of signatures. Even María and Mr. Singh, the janitor from school, signed it. Joselito's got two pages already. But that's okay, 'cause my mom explained that when you're fighting for a cause you shouldn't compete with your comrades. After we've got all the signatures, our final tactic will be a big protest right by Cedar.

"La batea" by Quilapayún begins to play. MANUELITA hears it and walks over to the trunk. She pulls out a sign that says, "Get Your Dirty Hands Off Cedar."

SLIDE: A sign that reads "Boycott Chilean Goods."

We're staying up late tonight, making these signs, 'cause tomorrow we're gonna protest outside of Safeway, 'cause they sell Chilean fruit.

MANUELITA takes the sign and a marker centre stage and works on her sign.

Joselito and me are taking this opportunity to make signs for the protest we're gonna have by Cedar. Lassie says she'll come protest too. She's never been to a protest so she's kind of excited. Everybody's here tonight: all the Chileans, and all the gringos too. The Chileans used to make fun of the gringos 'cause they dress funny, but my mom told the Chileans to shut the fuck up because the gringos had a big heart and were willing to do solidarity with a country they'd never even been to.

MANUELITA puts the sign and the marker back in the trunk and sits on it.

But the gringos do dress kind of funny. They have different coloured hair and stuff. My mom explained that they're from a thing called the Anarchist Movement, and the hippie ones are draft-dodgers she called them, from the U.S., and then she said that some are also from the Gay and Lesbian Movement. My dad got kinda red when she explained what gays and lesbians are, but she told him to grow up, so he didn't say anything. Ever since she explained what they were, I don't make Barbie and Ken kiss at Lassie's house. I practice with two Barbies kissing, it doesn't look so bad.

MANUELITA stands up, opens the trunk, and starts putting the pink nightgown on again.

I'm getting ready 'cause me, my mom, and Crespa are going to buy me a Barbie. Today is the first time we go to a store that's not the Salvation Army, even though lately we've been going to the Army and Navy, but that doesn't count, 'cause only immigrants go there. Today we're actually going to a mall, and my mom says we're gonna have lunch at McDonald's. Yay! I already know exactly which Barbie I want: the one with hair down to her knees. Her hair's kinda wavy, and she comes dressed with an evening gown and gold shoes. I already know what I'm gonna call her, too. Marsha. Marsha.

At the mall.

We find the aisle with all the Barbies on the shelves, just like at Lassie's house, and I see the one I want. I take her and study her closely. When I look up, my mom is holding a Barbie too. She walks up to me with it and says, "This one's perfect for you, Manuelita." Crespa's standing behind her, smiling.

MANUELITA faints. The "Faint Song" comes on.

The floor opens up and sucks me in, and down, down to the place where I go to as I lie awake at night, and my mind speaks to me in English. The world spins and my grandmother's face turns into a blur. I land in the schoolyard where I speak only English. In Lassie's house where I speak only English. The floor sucks me away from all this Chilean-ness.

MANUELITA gets up from the floor.

I look at the Barbie my mother has chosen: a Hawaiian dancer, complete with grass skirt and flower necklace. "Look, she's beautiful, Manuelita, just like you," says my mom, and she holds the Barbie up to my arm, "and she's got your skin colour." Crespa says, "You can call her María or Carmen." No Marsha. I have a knot in my throat now so I can't speak. I put Marsha back and walk to the cashier with the Hawaiian dancer. Marsha's skin was the colour of snow. This Barbie's skin, my skin, is the colour of shit.

"Island Girl" by Elton John begins to play.

MANUELITA takes off the pink nightgown and throws it into the trunk. She pulls the Hawaiian dancer Barbie out of the trunk and some white nail polish. She paints the Barbie's leg white, becomes frustrated with the results and starts to paint her own arms and hand white. She realizes this is not going to work, so she throws the Barbie and nail polish back into the trunk.

MANUELITA walks centre stage.

We all decided to do a big barbecue at Cates Park so everybody could celebrate and eat like pigs before the hunger strike. The Chileans are trying to teach Bill and the other gringos *cueca,* while I try and teach Joselito the hustle, that I learned yesterday at disco-dancing classes.

MANUELITA does a few steps from the hustle.

Joselito points and I see Crespa sneaking into the woods with Cachete, even though she's married to Titicaco. *Crespa and Cachete sitting in a tree, k-i-s-s-i-n-g! First comes love, then comes marriage, then comes Crespa and the baby carriage!*

There's a big group of people next to us. They don't speak English either, and my mom explains that they're from India and to stop staring. They're kinda loud. Just like us. I hear lots of noise, and I see a big group of Canadians coming. They got here on motorcycles, and all the ladies are wearing tight jeans and feathered hair, like Farrah Fawcett. They look nice. They set up their stuff and start looking at the people from India. They look and laugh and point. Some of them plug their noses and one of the men from India starts yelling at the Canadians, he's about to go and hit him, when all the other Indian men grab him and hold him back. The Canadians keep laughing, and now all the men are on their feet. I'm starting to feel sick, the hairs on the back of my neck rise and my knees are wobbly. Next thing I know, all the Chileans walk over to join the Indian people. Pelao is really mad, he starts swearing at the Canadians, "You kitchens! Kitchens! Kitchens! Kitchens!" and finally the Canadians leave.

MANUELITA sits on top of the desk.

For the rest of the day, we let people from India taste our food and we taste theirs, and they dance for us and we dance for them and everybody looks really happy, but all I feel is a big black emptiness, right here. And it hasn't gone away yet.

MANUELITA walks over to Cedar and climbs it. The "Letter Song" plays throughout.

SLIDE: A child's spelling test.

MANUELITA takes the clipboard and begins to write.

Querida Abuelita,

Ahora ya sé bailar el Car Wash, it's a disco dance, I wish I could show you the steps, Grandma. The other day we had a protest in front of the Chilean consulate and we let all the balloons go into the air and now all the adults are going on a hunger strike, but you don't have to worry 'cause they're gonna have a doctor check them every day. I wish I could go on the hunger strike but I'm too small and besides I have to go to school. I'm sending you my last spelling test. The gold star means that all my answers are right. I speak English good now but I still speak Spanish. Send hugs to all my aunts and uncles and cousins, and to Gabriela too, even though I haven't answered her last letter. Oh, well.

I love you, *Abuelita,*

Manuelita

"Canción de los C.D.R." by Silvio Rodríguez begins to play and MANUELITA goes and stands on the trunk.

SLIDE: A protest in Chile by the Mothers of the Disappeared.

Vomité, vomité, vomité ... Today's the first day of the hunger strike and everybody's here. There's even some Indigenous people beating on a drum to show their solidarity with us. The TV is here. All the Chileans are dressed real nice 'cause they're gonna be on TV, and Bill's gonna translate for everybody. Pelao's already talking about how hungry he is and the hunger strike hasn't started yet and Juan of the Chickens keeps talking about how sick he is of eating fried chicken and Calladita keeps elbowing him in the ribs, 'cause he's not supposed to talk about food in front of the strikers. My mom and dad are being interviewed. My father's face lights up for the camera, and Bill can barely keep up with the translating ... "We are here because we want the world to know that the Chilean people haven't laid down to die, that in spite of the unbridled murder, torture, and disappearances being carried out now against our *compañeros*, we, the exiles, continue to fight for our country, even from outside ..." My father's old voice, the one from before, comes to life and that old sparkle, the one he lost after the coup, the one that died when we came here, explodes into his eyes. His back straightens, his hands fly like birds and his smile shines like a piano. There is absolute silence as my father continues. I walk up to him, put an arm around his leg and my hand in his. I can smell his Colonia Inglesa, I can smell the *mil hojas* cake my grandmother made to bid us farewell, I can smell the diesel on the Alameda! I would give anything, anything, *anything* to go back now, maybe I can erase the marks on my parents' passports and nobody will notice. Maybe Joselito can help me, it will be our secret operation and we'll be blood brothers again for it.

"A Cochabamba me voy" by Víctor Jara begins to play.

SLIDE: A young Nicaraguan woman with a rifle slung on her shoulder. She's nursing a baby.

MANUELITA climbs onto the desk and plays at being a guerilla fighter; she looks around, ducks, hides, and so on.

Juan of the Chickens is telling us all about Tania, the guerilla, Che's right-hand woman in Bolivia.

MANUELITA runs to the trunk and crouches by it.

He's acting everything out for us as Calladita laughs and shakes her head.

MANUELITA sits on the trunk.

Juan of the Chickens and Calladita are in charge of all us kids during the hunger strike. We're all in our pyjamas and it's late. Every night Juan of the Chickens and Calladita take turns teaching us about the history of our people, they call it. They also teach us Spanish writing and reading 'cause we're kinda forgetting and they make us dance the *cueca* too. Then all us kids sleep in my room and Calladita sleeps in my parents' room and Juan of the Chickens in the living room. Tonight me and Joselito are gonna do another big operation. We're gonna wait till Calladita's asleep, then we're gonna sneak into my parents' room and take their passports. They're in the bottom dresser drawer.

MANUELITA lies on the trunk.

So me and Joselito are in my room. We make sure the other kids are asleep.

MANUELITA crawls upstage left and stays there, on her knees.

Then we crawl out of my room, into the hall and creep right into my parents' room. We can hear Juan of the Chickens snoring and talking in his sleep in the living room. We can't hear anything from Calladita, so we assume she's as quiet when she's sleeping as when she's awake. Joselito stands guard while I go through the drawer.

SLIDE: The cover of a Chilean passport.

I find the passports real easy.

MANUELITA crawls upstage right and stays on her knees.

We sneak into the bathroom, climb into the bathtub, and close the curtain. Joselito lights a match so I can look for the marks. I have no idea what these marks are supposed to look like –

SLIDE: The inside of the passport with a big "L" scrawled across it.

They're huge! They take up a whole page. It will take many nights' work to get rid of these marks, but we're willing to do it. Phase one of our operation is done.

MANUELITA gets up from the floor and walks to the desk. She sits on it.

I told Lassie that me and Joselito are urban guerillas. She promised not to tell anybody but then she got real excited so we started up our own urban guerilla group at school. We carry out secret operations.

SLIDE: "If You Go Into the Woods Today."

Me and Lassie recruited Catherine Suzanne and Yoko and Megan and Rashmi and a couple of other girls in the class. We decided our first operation would be to try and find the bad men in the woods that the policeman was talking about the day I pissed myself and screamed and ran away.

The sound of a buzzer.

MANUELITA goes downstage centre and drags herself along the floor, crossing upstage centre.

It's lunch time and we're all sneaking into the woods. We drag ourselves along the ground until we're finally in the forbidden zone.

MANUELITA stands up.

Today we're gonna try and make it down to the ravine, 'cause we'll find lots of clues down there and the bad men might be hiding there. The other girls nod. "Here's a clue," says Lassie. She holds up a twig for us all to inspect. "I bet the bad men stepped on it," I say, following Lassie's train of thought. All the other girls nod. I decide to keep this clue, so I put it in my pocket and we continue on our way. We find some scratches on a rock, and we realize the bad men must have sharpened their knives on it. We know we're getting close. They must be very near. We're gonna write the bad men a note and leave it hanging on this tree, just so they know they're dead. The others nod.

"Who's gonna write the note?" asks Yoko. It has to be someone who has boy's handwriting, so the bad men won't know it's us who wrote it. None of us has boy's handwriting, but Megan is the best choice 'cause she can fake the squiggliness of it really good. She writes: "Beware, bad men. We're gonna get you," and then she draws a skull. We hang the note on a tree right on the edge of the ravine.

The sound of a buzzer.

Lunch is over, comrades, we must make our way back.

MANUELITA skips over to the trunk and crouches by it.

I've decided that the girls from school are professional enough to help out with Cedar's protest.

MANUELITA takes out the Hawaiian dancer.

Any day now.

MANUELITA puts the Barbie underneath her T-Shirt, climbs over the trunk and makes her way to Cedar. She climbs it. She pulls the Barbie out, cautiously.

SLIDE: "Compartmentalized Struggle."

MANUELITA talks directly to the Barbie.

You can be my top-secret right-hand woman in this compartmentalized struggle.

"Oh, good."

Your political name will be Tania. But remember. You must live in hiding and break all contact with the world as you know it.

"Okay."

MANUELITA kisses the Barbie and hides her in the tree. She then climbs out of the tree and lands on the floor, on her knees.

Me and Joselito are back in the bathtub. It's around three in the morning and we've got some liquid paper that Joselito stole from his teacher's desk without anybody noticing, and now he's holding a match up to the passports while I blot out the big huge marks.

MANUELITA mimes blowing out the match and then covers her mouth.

We hear somebody coming out of Calladita's room. The person makes their way to the living room, where Juan of the Chickens is laughing in his sleep. Now Calladita's laughing too. Juan of the Chickens and Calladita moan and groan and sigh and talk in deep voices and we hear bodies moving and kissing sounds and rustling sheets. They're doing it! We wait until the moaning turns into loud vowel sounds and quickly climb out of the bathtub and hit the decks in our room. We both know that this is another one of our secrets and that we are blood brothers once again.

MANUELITA stands up.

SLIDE: Pictures of the disappeared with candles around them.

My mom and dad look kinda skinny. It's been two weeks now of just water and they have to drag themselves to the bathroom 'cause they can't stand. Everybody's lying around and now that us kids are here they wanna know exactly what we've eaten. So I start telling them how I found twenty-five cents so I got a Revello, and everybody moans –

MANUELITA walks over to the trunk and starts putting on a frilly nightgown and sheer housecoat over it.

– and Joselito tells about eating the *cazuela* that Calladita and Juan of the Chickens make and everybody moans again and Juan of the Chickens tells about the fried chicken he eats and everybody moans again and he says there's no reason to moan 'cause it tastes like shit. Just then Crespa turns the TV on and there's a chicken commercial and everybody moans again.

Juan of the Chickens announces that today is a very special day 'cause us kids have prepared a play to entertain the strikers and get their minds off fucking food.

MANUELITA stands on the trunk. Fairy-tale music accompanies the following line.

This play is called *Cinderella*.

MANUELITA lies back on the trunk, miming holding a cigarette.

"Oh, Cinderella, have you dusted the picture of the Virgin that's hanging up over my bed yet?"

MANUELITA walks around, miming smoking.

"Well, don't just stand there like a *rota* and remember to starch the bow on my poodle's head, poor thing."

MANUELITA does two spins.

"I've got Pituca right here, stepmother. I'll also give her a bath in salts too, just like you asked."

MANUELITA walks, smoking.

"The ball is going to be magnificent, girls. Marble floors and crystal chandeliers like you've never seen ..."

MANUELITA leans on the desk and has a huge coughing fit. She horks.

"And royalty: dukes, counts, princes. Choose well girls, choose well."

MANUELITA puts a black sock on each hand and crouches behind the desk, doing puppets.

"Of course, mother."

"We would never disappoint you."

MANUELITA spins.

"May I go to the ball too, stepmother?"

MANUELITA walks, smoking.

"Hee-hee. Did you hear that, girls? This *rota piojosa* wants to go to the ball. Once you've washed and waxed all the floors, plucked the chickens, taken care of all the mouse traps, finished embroidering that tablecloth, milked the cows, and re-planted the orchard, maybe I'll let you go to the ball, silly. Hee, hee."

MANUELITA has a huge coughing fit and horks. She waves.

"Bye-bye! Have a nice time at the ball!"

MANUELITA starts crying and collapses onto the floor as she cleans it with her nightgown.

We hear fairy godmother music.
MANUELITA stands up, very erect.

"Don't cry, little one. You don't need to take this exploitation from the bourgeoisie. Come join me in the struggle for the proletariat and fight for a more just society, comrade."

MANUELITA goes back to the floor.

"But who are you?"

MANUELITA stands up again, holding out the housecoat as if it were a cape.

"I am Tania, the guerilla. And that over there is Che."

MANUELITA takes two steps to the side and holds up her left fist.

"*Hasta la victoria siempre.*"

MANUELITA spins.

"Nice to meet you."

MANUELITA holds her cape out. "Come with us. We're up there, in the mountains. And bring that chicken while you're at it. We're starving."

MANUELITA spins.

"But what about my stepmother?"

MANUELITA holds her cape out.

"Fuck her."

"Trabajdores al poder" by ¡Karaxú! begins to play as MANUELITA takes her costume off

and bows. She puts it in the trunk and takes out her "Keep Your Dirty Hands Off Cedar" sign.

"*¡Trabajadores trampolé! ¡Trabajadores trampolé!*"

MANUELITA goes up her tree.

Everybody's here. Joselito and all the other kids and Lassie and the other girls from school.

MANUELITA puts the sign around her neck.

Everybody from the neighbourhood is coming around to see what we're doing and Lassie is explaining about how poor Cedar is going to be chopped down to make a house. They all have petitions and people are signing them. I see Bill. He's coming with the people from the TV! Everybody's jumping up and down with excitement and Lassie keeps yelling, "Look, Monoleeda! Look! The TV's here!"

I wanna climb down from my tree but Joselito points out that the protest will be stronger if I just stay up here with my sign. The TV people are filming all of us and Bill is talking to them. Now they're interviewing Joselito and Lassie, who are my spokespeople, and the cameraman is filming me!

MANUELITA waves at the TV, with a big smile on her face. She then regains her composure and becomes very serious, pointing to her sign. She holds up her left fist.

More and more people from the neighbourhood are coming and the tractor people are just getting back from their lunch break. They look kind of shocked.

"Get your dirty hands off Cedar! Don't touch Cedar!"

SLIDE: Two little Chilean girls at school. This later dissolves into a slide of Valparaíso.

MANUELITA starts to read a postcard.
The "Letter Song" plays throughout.

Queridísima Manuela,

¿Cómo lo estás pasando en Canadá? Debe haber mucha nieve y todo debe ser muy blanco. I miss you. At school, there's nobody there to sing the Chilean national anthem with me anymore, there's nobody to sit beside and giggle at Señorita Negretti's moustache with. Your grandma is really sad that you're gone. She says she never thought it would be so long.

I still play with the doll you left for me to take care of till you came back, and every day I wear that necklace that we made out of buttons and I dream about you every night. Do you like the postcard? See how Valparaíso is the same as when you left?

Hugs and kisses,
Gabriela

P.S. Doña Olvido from the vegetable store says hi and so does Don Pablo from the bakery.

MANUELITA shows the postcard to her Barbie.

I wish she'd send me a picture of herself, Tania. I barely remember what she looks like.

"El Pueblo Unido Jamás Será Vencido" by Inti-Illimani begins to play. MANUELITA hears it and climbs down from Cedar. She stands stage right and ends up sitting on the trunk.

SLIDE: The Mothers of the Disappeared protesting in Chile.

The hunger strike is finally over and everybody's here, celebrating. Even the doctor that took care of everybody. He's Palestinian and my mom explained that he went to check the strikers for free, 'cause he and his Palestinian friends are in solidarity with us. All the adults are hugging and kissing me and Joselito and the other kids 'cause they saw us on TV. My mom and dad are real proud of me. I can tell from the way they're talking about me to the other adults. The doctor's making sure nobody pigs out, but Pelao and Gordo have already made themselves an eighteen-egg omelette and are eating it straight out of the pan. My mom and dad look happy 'cause they say the hunger strike was a success. But I don't really get it 'cause the disappeared are still disappeared, but they explained this thing to me about raising awareness or something like that. Some of the adults are worried 'cause they lost their jobs while they were on strike, but everybody's still eating and drinking and telling jokes when we get a call from Chile. My mom answers and everybody gathers around.

MANUELITA stands up. The sound of a dial tone starts and gets louder and louder throughout the next section.

My mom gets less and less happy. Her mouth drops open and she drops the phone. My dad picks it up and he just shakes his head as he listens and says, "Ayayay." Finally he hangs up.

My grandmother is dead.

MANUELITA runs to Cedar and climbs it.

SLIDE: Grandmother; it dissolves into Chilean women gathered in protest in Chile.

My mom phoned the Chilean consul and begged him to give her a twenty-four permit to go to Valparaíso to bury my grandmother. The consul said, "Over my dead body you fucking Communist bitch." I just sit here. Keeping Cedar company. My parents and the other adults always say we kids don't remember anything, but right now I'm on the train to Santiago with my grandmother and we're buying *churros* at the Cerro Santa Lucía ... (*singing*) *caballito blanco llévame de aquí, llévame a mi pueblo donde yo nací, tengo, tengo, tengo, tú no tienes nada ...*

MANUELITA slowly pulls the blonde wig off and fixes her hair. She looks at her hand holding the wig in her lap and hides her hand behind her back, covering the white nail polish.

When my mother begged the consul to go and bury her mother, I showed her the passports, I told her that I'd gotten rid of the marks so she could go, but she just cried harder and said, "You poor thing," so I hugged her.

MANUELITA looks straight ahead. She climbs down from the tree and starts tying herself to Cedar with a rope.

Calladita told me about the Mothers and Wives of the Disappeared chaining themselves to the Presidential Palace in Chile.

MANUELITA finishes tying herself and then puts her sign on.

The tractors are coming. Straight for Cedar.

MANUELITA stares straight ahead, ready. The lights go black and a single headlight shines onto her face from downstage left.

"Al final de este viaje en la vida" by Isabel Parra begins to play.

The song plays in its entirety, through the walkout.

The End.

¿QUE PASA WITH LA RAZA, EH?

CARMEN AGUIRRE
AND THE LATINO THEATRE GROUP

for the disappeared

PRODUCTION HISTORY

¿QUE PASA with LA RASA, eh? premiered as a co-production between Headlines Theatre Company and the Firehall Arts Centre in Vancouver, British Columbia, from March 18 to 27, 1999, with the following cast and crew:

SKIN
and secondary characters — Kenia Avendaño

DANDELION
and secondary characters — Itzel Bazerque-Patrich

SOMBRA
and secondary characters — Wendy Méndez

RATA
and secondary characters — Angelo Moroni

ZAP
and secondary characters — Oparin Ortiz

JULIO
and secondary characters — Rocco Trigueros

Director — Carmen Aguirre
Choreographer — Barbara Bourget
Set Designer — James Fagan Tait
Lighting Designer — Eduardo Meneses
Sound Designer — Alejandro Verdecchia
Costume Designer — Tyler Tone
Slide Designer — Tim Matheson
Stage Manager — Kerrene John

¿QUE PASA with LA RAZA, eh? was co-written by Carmen Aguirre and the following members of the Latino Theatre Group: Kenia Avendaño, Eduardo Azmitia, Itzel Bazerque-Patrich, Wendy Méndez, Angelo Moroni, Francisca Varas, and Eduardo Villaseñor.

It was dramaturged by Chapelle Jaffe of the Playwrights Theatre Centre in Vancouver. The play could not have been devised without the financial assistance of the Canada Council for the Arts and the City of Vancouver through its Diversity Initiatives Program.

PRODUCTION NOTES AND SETTING

The play's main setting is East Vancouver, 1999.

The stage is bare and dominated by a huge, white, upside-down map of Latin America suspended at the back of the stage. The various locales of the play are conveyed by slides projected onto this canvas, as well as by sound and lighting.

The stage is painted black and looks like an abandoned warehouse that has been taken over by the play's group of young people who are telling their stories. There are no curtains or blacks; pipes, cables, speakers, and lighting equipment are exposed. All the props and costumes are visible, placed on tables and hung on racks against the left or right walls.

The cast never leaves the stage. When a cast member is "offstage" they sit to the side on a crate or box and witness the action. The cast wears a basic costume that can be added to. Different characters are created with a hat, a bandana, a shirt layered over the basic costume, a prop.

A choreographer is essential for the play's three dance numbers: at the top of the play, before Skin's "Rainbow Nation" speech, and at the end of the play. These dance numbers are hip-hop with a little breakdancing thrown in. The transitions should also be choreographed as dance numbers, and the romantic scene between Zap and Skin at the restaurant should be choreographed to El Vez's "Fever," ending in a kiss.

CHARACTERS

The thirty characters in this play can be performed by six actors.

To be played by one actor:
ZAP, twenty years old
SANTO, in his twenties
CHACHO, in his thirties
DEATH SQUAD MEMBER
RAINBOW NATION STUDENT UNION MEMBER

To be played by one actor:
RATA, twenty-five years old
SOMBRA'S DAD, thirty years old
RAINBOW NATION STUDENT UNION MEMBER

To be played by one actor:
SOMBRA, twenty years old
LUZ, twenty years old
VIRGIN GUADALUPE
UNDOCUMENTED TRUCK PASSENGER
RAINBOW NATION STUDENT UNION MEMBER

To be played by one actor:
SKIN, twenty years old
MÓNICA SONORA DINAMITA, in her forties
GRACIELA, eleven years old
SOMBRA'S MOM, thirty years old
UNDOCUMENTED TRUCK PASSENGER

To be played by one actor:
DANDELION, twenty years old
FEDERICO, in his twenties
VERÓNICA (Graciela's mother), in her early thirties
DEATH SQUAD MEMBER
UNDOCUMENTED TRUCK PASSENGER
RAINBOW NATION STUDENT UNION MEMBER

To be played by one actor:
JULIO, thirty years old
EDUARDO, in his thirties
FATHER JOSEPH, in his sixties
JUAN (Graciela's father, Veronica's husband), in his early thirties
RODRIGO, in his early twenties
RAINBOW NATION STUDENT UNION MEMBER

PROLOGUE

A slide with the text "South America" written upside down is projected onto a huge, white, upside-down map of Latin America hanging at the back of the stage.

"Never Been to Spain" by El Vez begins to play as house lights slowly start to dim. As the first verse of the song finishes with the line "In 1492 who discovered who, here's how it happened," the house is black, the stage is black, and the music cuts out, immediately followed by "Mexican Power" by Proper Dos at full blast as the lights come up on the entire cast dancing over-the-top hip-hop. They may also breakdance. In the prologue, the actors play themselves (members of the Latino Theatre Group), not their main characters. As they dance, slides come up on the screen. The text on the slides is in speech bubbles, like a comic strip, and is interspersed with images from the Love and Rockets *comic books.*

Slide #1: "The Firehall Arts Centre and Headlines Theatre Company present the Latino Theatre Group in ¿QUE PASA with *LA RAZA,* eh?*"*

Slide #2: "The Latino Theatre Group was created in 1994 to express our Latino selves through theatre."

Slide #3: "Five years later, we just can't seem to stop expressing ourselves."

Slide #4: "We're a soulful bunch, full of Latino pride and lots of stories to share with you."

Slide #5: "Like, did you know that none of us are actors? No! We're all, like, journalists and cashiers and child-care workers and high-school students and college students and computer geeks and so on and so on and so on."

Slide #6: "In other words we're the real thing from the real Vancouver Latino community here to tell you some real stories based on our real selves."

Slide #7: "Welcome to the Firehall, on the Downtown Eastside of Vancouver, in the northwestern tip of the Americas, this continent that contains us all."

Slide #8: "And remember, don't call us Hispanic, 'cause we ain't never been to Spain."

Slide #9: "If anything, call us Americans, 'cause we are all from the Americas."

The cast dances offstage as the final slide dissolves, except for the actor playing SANTO. He transforms into SANTO and approaches the audience to deliver his monologue to them. He carries a flashlight.

ACT ONE

SCENE ONE

SANTO: Welcome to the fabulous Rio Grande and behold its crystal-blue splendour as it runs here before your very eyes. This river stretches from east to west, but what is important to us lies north, north across the Rio Grande, nestled in those lush, green, rolling hills.

Now ladies and gentlemen, this is no ordinary river. Oh no! This Rio Grande will take you, as it has taken many before you, to a land of great opportunity and wealth, yes, riches beyond your wildest dreams. Your decision to cross this river, with my guidance and expertise, of course, will change your destiny and life as you embark into the next millennium in the North: Eden.

I ask, can you imagine a land with no twelve-hour lineups? Now you will be able to pay a phone bill sitting at home, through what's called a computer, the internet – I know you don't know what that means – the internet. Everyone in the North has a computer.

Can you fathom a place where the streets are impeccable, where you don't have to be worried about walking over feces and rotting garbage? In the North, the sidewalks are so clean you can literally eat off them. And there's clean water; you don't need to boil it, and – I kid you not – central heating.

But that's only the beginning. Everyone in the North has or can find a job. Everyone. Everyone is employed. They have positions for – don't laugh, this is serious – they have positions as turkey watchers at supermarkets at Christmas time. You can get a job waxing apples. Anything and everything. They will find a job for you, you need not worry.

That's not the best part. This is the best part: I'll tell you about the people. The people are all beautiful. Tall, blonde, blue eyes, you know, picturesque, romanesque, you know, in an uncanny kind of way. Gorgeous. And you, with this job, being a turkey-watcher or an apple-waxer, you can pay to be blonde and blue-eyed as well. More important, however, is how nice these people are.

Here in the South, when you walk down the street, people stare you down, or are rude or pushy. In the North, people are always smiling, they walk around with name tags and they even stop to say, "Hi! How are you!" And they mean it.

Oh, once I get started talking about the North I can't stop. I could stand here for hours, tickled pink, describing the North to you.

And so, without further ado, allow me to introduce myself. Now I have many names. I have been called guide, messenger, coyote, messiah. But, uh, you can call me Santo.

A slide appears, saying: "One swim south of the border, 1996." SANTO walks stage left, with his flashlight on. The RIVER CROSSERS – VERÓNICA, JUAN, LUZ, and GRACIELA, with RATA – are lined up, ready to go. SANTO shines the flashlight on their faces throughout the next sequence.

SANTO: (*to VERÓNICA*) You already paid? (*grabbing VERÓNICA's face and studying it closely with his flashlight*) I don't recognize you.

VERÓNICA pulls away.

SANTO: Hey! Watch yourself!

JUAN: Leave her alone.

SANTO: Was I talking to you? (*to VERÓNICA*) Did you pay?

VERÓNICA: Yes.

SANTO: (*to LUZ*) What's your name?

LUZ: Luz.

SANTO: Luz what?

LUZ: Muñóz. My uncle paid you.

SANTO: What's his name?

LUZ: Mario.

SANTO: Okay. Everybody give me your jewelry, your wallets, anything precious and heavy … now hurry up. We don't have time to waste.

VERÓNICA: We already paid you.

SANTO: It's for safekeeping. Just hand it over. I don't have time to waste. I'm gonna get you across safely and I'm gonna take care of your stuff. Now, if we can do this fast, we're not gonna have any problem.

SANTO takes all the RIVER CROSSERS' valuables, including jewelry they are wearing. He finishes by taking a chain off RATA's neck.

RATA: My mother's –

SANTO: What's your name?

RATA: Rata.

SANTO: Ratas don't have mothers.

LUZ: We already paid. You don't need our stuff –

SANTO: Due to out-of-control inflation the currency devalued. Okay. We're gonna cross the water. First, everybody take off your clothes. Now.

VERÓNICA: What?

SANTO: Take off your clothes!

JUAN: Ladies too?

SANTO: Everybody take off your clothes! I don't have time to waste! Let's go.

RATA begins to take off his clothes.

VERÓNICA: Why didn't you tell us this in the first place?

SANTO: Listen, do you wanna get across? Do you fucking wanna get across?

The rest of the RIVER CROSSERS start to take off their clothes.

GRACIELA: It's freezing.

SANTO: Listen. I don't give a shit if it's freezing, okay? When you cross this river and get to the other side and the local authorities see that you are dripping with water, they're gonna label you a fucking wetback. And do you know what they're gonna do? They're gonna take you and your raggedy-ass friends to prison. And the dogs are gonna tear you limb from limb. And they'll ship you here and you know what they're gonna do to you here. The shit we can't even talk about.

LUZ: Well, what about you? You're gonna get us caught then if you don't take your clothes off.

SANTO: You and me will worry about that later, baby ... okay. In a single-file line. Nobody make a sharp movement, nobody fucking make a noise, understand? Let's go.

SANTO leads the single file line of RIVER CROSSERS to the edge of the river. They hold their bundles above their heads as they step into the water and begin to cross.

GRACIELA: Oh, it's cold.

SANTO: Shut the fuck up!

VERÓNICA: It's too deep.

SANTO: Shut up.

Searchlights begin to appear.

GRACIELA: There's a rat ... there's lights!

SANTO: Shut up. Shut her up.

GRACIELA and VERÓNICA start to scream.

RATA: Shut the fuck up! I wanna fucking get across!

The searchlights come on full force along with the overpowering sounds of helicopters and dogs.

LUZ: (*as the searchlights come on*) I can hear the dogs! There's lights! There's lights!

SANTO: Shit, lights ... helicopters! Get down! Get down!

SANTO and the RIVER CROSSERS go underwater, and, in slow motion, begin to be swept away by the current.

Lights change: We are now entering the RIVER CROSSERS' hopes and dreams. Each RIVER CROSSER speaks as they continue to be carried by the current in slow motion.

VERÓNICA: Before you know it we'll be there, daughter mine. Before you know it you'll be full of friends in your new school and I'll be working the harvest in a land that used to be ours ... before you know it ... be strong, daughter mine ... in a land that used to be ours ...

JUAN: Goodbye to the land that saw me being born and become a man, goodbye to the land that I have loved until death do us part. Goodbye, beloved Mexico ... Virgin Guadalupe, I implore you to take care of my wife and daughter in our new land ... my wife and daughter ...

GRACIELA: ... Mamá ... Papá ...

LUZ: Integrity ... I will not betray you ... I will become a journalist and keep the memory of Chiapas alive ...

RATA: Guatemala is a million miles away now ... one border crossed, two more to go ... the North beckons as the South dissolves, burning a hole in my heart ...

The lights change back to reality. Some time has passed. The RIVER CROSSERS emerge at the other side of the river. They pull up on all fours, out of breath and in despair. The helicopter and dogs can be heard far away. GRACIELA, amid coughs and screams, looks around to find that JUAN and VERÓNICA are missing.

GRACIELA: Mamá! Papá! Mamá! Papá!!

Gathering himself, SANTO fumbles with the flashlight.

SANTO: Shut up! They'll hear you!

GRACIELA: Mamá!! (*getting up and running around, desperately looking in all directions*) Papá!!

SANTO: I am telling you to shut the fuck up.

GRACIELA: Oh my God! They're gone! Gone!! They're dead! The river took them! Mamá!! Papá!! They're dead!

SANTO: And you'll be dead too unless you shut up. We're lucky we made it this far. Now just shut your mouth and we can keep going.

RATA starts to get dressed, preparing himself for the next leg of the journey. GRACIELA starts to wail. LUZ becomes hysterical and has an out-of-control laugh attack.

SANTO: Holy shit. Listen. It is very important that you shut the fuck up. I don't know how else to put it. You don't know what they're capable of ... what they'll do if they catch us ... you don't know this border ... you have got to shut the fuck up before I fucking kill you ...

GRACIELA's wailing continues. LUZ's laughter gets higher in pitch and louder. She is truly out of control.

SANTO: You fucking bitch. Shut up before I kill you ...

SANTO runs around, trying to figure out what to do, intermittently searching the sky and horizon for lights, helicopters, and dogs. RATA is ready to go. GRACIELA and LUZ continue wailing and laughing.

SANTO: That's it. I don't wanna leave you ladies alone here but unless you stop the fucking noise I'm gonna have to take off without you. Hear me?

GRACIELA and LUZ continue wailing and laughing.

SANTO: (*to LUZ*) You fucking bitch.

He walks over to her.

SANTO: Shut up.

SANTO grabs LUZ's shoulders and shakes her.

SANTO: Shut the fuck up.

SANTO continues to shake LUZ. LUZ continues laughing. SANTO punches LUZ in the face. LUZ falls. SANTO looks around. SANTO rapes LUZ. GRACIELA continues wailing. RATA looks away.

RODRIGO and FEDERICO, two U.S. border guards, enter the scene, waving guns. RATA hides behind a bush and remains unseen for the rest of the scene.

FEDERICO: (*pointing his gun*) Freeze! U.S. Immigration! You are all under arrest! You get those, Rodrigo, I'll get the other one.

RODRIGO: (*kicking SANTO in the face, throwing him off LUZ*) Sorry to interrupt, lover boy.

RODRIGO rounds up LUZ and SANTO, placing them on their knees, hands behind their heads.

FEDERICO: (*to GRACIELA*) Get over here, you fucking lettuce-picker. Now!

FEDERICO places GRACIELA on her knees, hands behind her head. Now GRACIELA, SANTO, and LUZ are in a line, on their knees, hands behind their heads, as RODRIGO and FEDERICO threaten them with their guns.

RODRIGO: (*into a walkie-talkie*) Three more, boss. Oh yeah, fresh, fresh, fresh off the boat, dripping wet, right Federico? No, these are definitely alive and kicking, not like those other ones we found down the river, the place is crawling with them – yeah, we'll bring them right over. (*to FEDERICO*) Three down and it's only our first hour.

FEDERICO grabs SANTO's hair as he puts his gun against his head. SANTO has been trying to inch away.

FEDERICO: One move and you're dead, shitheads.

GRACIELA: Mami –

LUZ: Federico, you're one of us –

FEDERICO: Say my name again, grease-head, and you'll be sorry –

LUZ: But you're one of us, both of you, are just like us, we all belong to the same race, you're not gringos, you're Latinos just like us and you should be ashamed –

RODRIGO: What the fuck's this wetback going on about? Are you calling us wetbacks?

LUZ: I was just trying to point out that you are Latinos just like us and you should be ashamed –

RODRIGO: We are American citizens and proud of it. Born and raised. One more word out of any of you and we'll set you on fire. Let's go.

FEDERICO: On your feet, darkies. Let's go.

GRACIELA: Mami –

LUZ: We have done nothing wrong –

RODRIGO: Oh, you only tried to enter the United States of America illegally –

LUZ: This land is ours and it was taken from us –

GRACIELA, SANTO, LUZ, FEDERICO, and RODRIGO all file offstage. RATA remains behind his bush. He comes out, looks around, kisses a rosary that he fishes out of his pocket, and starts running to the sound of full-blast Brazilian batucada. RATA looks into the horizon. The day is starting to break. He keeps running.

SCENE TWO

It is now noon, and boiling hot. RATA is trudging along a southern California highway.

EDUARDO enters, driving his truck, which is formed by the cast members playing undocumented truck passengers walking behind him as he mimes driving. EDUARDO spots RATA walking along the highway and stops. The batucada cuts out.

EDUARDO: Hey! *Hermano*! *Compadre*!

RATA pretends not to notice EDUARDO and keeps walking.

EDUARDO: Hey! *Compadre*! Brother!

RATA pretends not to notice EDUARDO and keeps walking.

EDUARDO: Hey! You're gonna melt in this heat.

RATA keeps ignoring EDUARDO.

EDUARDO: A lone illegal walking down the highway ... you're lucky I'm not with the migra. If I was you I'd get in my truck before you end up in the slammer and back where you came from.

RATA stops. He looks around. He fidgets.

EDUARDO: Come on, *compadrito*. We all look out for each other here. Hurry it up before you get your ass kicked all the way back south ... you've come this far. You don't wanna blow it now. You managed to cross the most heavily guarded border in the Americas and now you're walking down this highway like you're on a Sunday stroll around the plaza ... Where you headed?

RATA: Canada.

EDUARDO: Relatives there?

RATA: No, I just need a new land.

EDUARDO: Well, hop right in. I can take you as far as San Diego. Then you're on your own. Just follow the coast. Get on trains. Hitch rides. I hear you can pretty well walk right into Canada. Easy border.

RATA walks toward the passenger side of the truck.

EDUARDO: I gotta hand it to you. Getting through this border in one piece and then walking along here like Dorothy following the Yellow Brick Road. Might as well be wearing a sign on your back: "I just swam across the border. I got no papers. Take me while I'm fresh." Get in.

RATA starts to open the door of the truck.

EDUARDO: No.

EDUARDO points to the back of the truck. RATA starts to move toward the back of the truck.

EDUARDO: (*making a gesture for money*) Hey.

RATA fishes in his pocket for the rosary and hands it to EDUARDO.

EDUARDO: We're all in this together, brother. *¡Viva la raza!*

RATA walks to the back of the truck. A bunch of hands emerge and pull him into the truck. EDUARDO starts to drive. Again the sound of batucada.

Time passes.

CHACHO, a California highway patrolman, appears. He waves the truck to a halt. The music stops.

CHACHO: (*approaching EDUARDO*) Good afternoon, sir. Can I see your green card, driver's license, and your registration papers, please.

EDUARDO: (*getting out of his truck*) Chacho! It's me! Your cousin!

CHACHO: Eduardo! Gotta tell you, this heat wave makes me deaf, dumb, and blind to the world. How are you?

EDUARDO: Oh, you know, driving, driving, always driving.

CHACHO : I heard on *Culture Clash FM* that this is the worst heat in forty years.

EDUARDO: No!

CHACHO: Yeah! And I'm stuck here like a mirage in the desert, waving at anything that moves.

EDUARDO: How's the old lady?

CHACHO: Oh, you know, working, working, always working.

EDUARDO: And the kids?

CHACHO: Oh, you know, playing, playing, always playing.

The truck passengers begin to faint,
one by one, from the heat.

CHACHO: What's all that noise?

EDUARDO: The watermelons.

CHACHO: That loud?

EDUARDO: Oh, yeah! You should see these watermelons. You know, with all that stuff they inject into them, they're this big! You wouldn't believe it!

CHACHO: That sounds really loud.

EDUARDO: Oh, it's the crates you know. Big honkin' crates with big honkin' watermelons.

CHACHO: How is the fruit business?

EDUARDO: Oh, you know, fruitful, fruitful, always fruitful.

CHACHO: Spare a watermelon? All this talk has my mouth watering –

CHACHO starts to walk to the back of the truck.

EDUARDO: They're all hammered into the crates. I'll bring you one. (*pulling CHACHO back toward the front of the truck*) So. You gonna set me up with your sister-in-law or what?

CHACHO: Cecilia? Are you crazy? Why would Miss Chicana '96 want to have anything to do with you? She can have any guy she wants. In fact, I heard that Jimmy Smits is thinking of asking her on a date –

EDUARDO: Aw, come on, what does she want with some movie star who's more worried about his ass than hers. Come on. I may be poor but I'm a hard worker, down to earth, and I've got good genes. We'll make beautiful children together.

CHACHO: I dunno...

EDUARDO: Bring her to Aunt Juana's barbecue on Sunday.

CHACHO: I'll think about it.

EDUARDO: You going to the barbecue?

CHACHO: It's the little one's Saint day, so we'll go after mass and bring the piñata.

EDUARDO: Bring Cecilia along. I'll be there in my Sunday best.

CHACHO: That's a lot of noise you got in that truck.

EDUARDO: Oh, God, look at the time. I'll be late with my shipment. Gotta go, I'll bring you a crate of watermelons on Sunday if you bring Cecilia.

CHACHO: Okay, okay. I should have checked your registration and your truck, they say the place is crawling with illegals –

By this point all the passengers have fainted from the heat, except RATA, who remains standing.

He creeps out of the truck and slowly makes his way offstage, unseen by CHACHO and EDUARDO.

EDUARDO: We're family, cousin. We all watch out for each other. (*climbing into the truck*) See ya on Sunday and *viva la raza*!

CHACHO: You sound like a homeboy.

Lights fade as "I Like It" by the Blackout All Stars begins to play.

SCENE THREE

A slide comes up on the screen. It says: "One swim, many rides, trains, hikes, and close calls: two borders later, 1999."

DANDELION stands on a chair centre stage, wearing an impromptu wedding dress and veil. SKIN and SOMBRA stand on either side of DANDELION, hemming the dress. RATA paces back and forth, downstage, talking into a cellphone. Music cuts out.

RATA: A lowrider limo. Yes that's what I want. You see the thing is, I want your best lowrider limo you have. Yeah I want hydraulics. Yes. Gold-plated. With boom system: everything ... yeah I have the fucking money. See the thing is that I wanna take it, drive it all the way down to Chile, so that I can have a limo business down there ... yeah, everyone's gonna wanna drive my limo ... yeah, man, everybody, the President, soccer stars ... yeah. I have the fucking money. See the thing now in Chile now is that it's advanced there ... yeah. They're First World now. They're not like those fucking Third World bastards around them. No, I'm not Chilean, I'm a man of the world ... yeah, so remember, I want a lowrider limo, yeah, that's right.

SKIN: Get off the fucking phone!

SKIN pulls the phone out of RATA's hand. They begin to physically struggle for the phone.

RATA: Here, here.

SKIN: No, Rata!

RATA: Give me my phone.

SKIN: No, Rata! Get off! Get off the phone!

RATA: Give me my phone. Give me my phone.

SOMBRA: Rata, every time you use that phone the CIA knows where you are.

RATA: Here.

SKIN: Rata, no.

RATA: Okay I don't wanna. I'm not playing. I'm not playing.

SKIN: No, no, no. Rata, obviously, you don't know what the hell is going on around here.

RATA: Yes I know, okay?

SKIN: No, no, no. Do you know what is going –

RATA: Yes, I know you have my phone and I want it back.

SKIN: Rata, this is a piece-of-shit phone. We have a phone here.

SOMBRA: Leave him alone –

SKIN: Why are you paying forty cents a second, a minute?

RATA: Because I can walk around. I get nervous.

SKIN: You're a fool.

RATA: I'm not a fool. Here. Give me the phone.

SKIN: No, no, no. You obviously don't know what the fuck is going on because, okay, until two days ago we thought you were here with your papers, man. With your papers. We thought you were legal here. Then you come to us and they gave you a deportation notice? Give me the fucking letter. Rata, you know, I am not your mother, okay? I am not your mother, but obviously you need a mother. I'm not your mother, the phone's not your mother – do you want me to read you the letter again?

RATA: Sure, I don't care.

SKIN: Give me the fucking letter.

RATA: Okay. Give me the fucking phone.

SKIN: The letter, man!

RATA: Give me the phone.

SKIN: Why are you such a boy?

RATA: Simple: phone, letter.

RATA and SKIN struggle one last time, until SKIN gives up the phone.

SKIN: You're wasting your time talking on an idiotic phone when you're gonna be deported in a month. Talking about buying a limo with a pool? Have you gone loopy? You're lucky I've got a soft spot for you, man, otherwise I'd have to turn you in to the loony bin. Take your stupid phone. I am going to read you the letter saying you violated Canada's Immigration Act because obviously you have no idea. No idea what the fuck sacrifice, us, your friends, are gonna do for you. Okay? This is on Canadian Government

Federal Immigration letterhead. That's important shit. "Dear Mr. Sandoval –"

SOMBRA: That's you, Rata.

SKIN: "We have been notified of your illegal stay" – you know, I can't even read this –

SOMBRA: In other words, you're getting deported.

SKIN: You are going to be deported.

SOMBRA: One month, man.

RATA: I fucked up, okay?

SKIN: Yeah, you fucked up, Rata. You know how bad you fucked up? Is that we're gonna get Dandelion, Granola – what's your name this week?

DANDELION: I'm sorry, but it's Dandelion.

SKIN: Why does she change it so many times?

DANDELION: I don't change it so many times. My name is Dandelion.

SKIN: Dandelion. Fuck. Dandelion is gonna pose as your wife.

RATA: I'm sorry, man. What can I do, okay? Thank you, thank you. I'm sorry. I'm a fucking man, okay?

SKIN: You're not a man. You're a little boy, man. That's why we always have to take care of you. Rata, you have no clue. Get with the program, okay? Get with the program. Geez. You don't understand –

There is a knock on the door.

SOMBRA: Okay, I'll get it.

SKIN: Rata, you're a fool, okay? You're a loser and you're a fool –

ZAP enters, singing and dancing.

ZAP: Going to the chapel and we're gonna get married –

SOMBRA: Shhh. Keep it down, Zap, my uncle's upstairs. You're gonna wake him up.

ZAP: I pulled a few strings.

SKIN: What?

ZAP: I'm so fuckin' stoked right now. Rata, Dandelion will be your wife. I talked Father Joseph into marrying you guys, as an act of solidarity. He's willing to marry you guys in the next month. Everything's set. You're getting married, man.

DANDELION: I'm sorry. Wait a second. You guys. Marriage? No no no no.

SOMBRA: You can get divorced in a year.

DANDELION: No. You guys never said anything about marriage. I'm not marrying him. I have a boyfriend.

SKIN: Yeah, but he's, you know, open-minded, he's Canadian. They're not jealous –

RATA: I'm not jealous –

DANDELION: I'm sorry. I have a boyfriend and I'm committed to him and you guys said pictures. Pictures –

SOMBRA: I know, but we –

DANDELION: Not marriage! No! How the hell did we get marriage from pictures?

SOMBRA: Well, we thought that the pictures wouldn't be enough, so –

SKIN: You just have to live under the same roof for a year –

DANDELION: Are you crazy? For a year? That's a whole year. No!

SOMBRA: You're the only one that can marry him, okay?

DANDELION: Why don't you do it, man?

SOMBRA: I'm going back to Guatemala in four months –

DANDELION: Why don't you do it? You're a Canadian citizen –

SKIN: You don't ask that question. You did not ask me that question – no no no. Excuse me.

SOMBRA: No, you guys.

SKIN: Step aside. Step to the fucking side, Sombra.

RATA: Here we go.

SKIN: No. Granola. Dandelion.

DANDELION: Dandelion's my name, thank you.

SKIN: Dandelion.

DANDELION: Yes.

SKIN: Dandelion!

DANDELION: Yes!

SKIN: How many times do I have to tell you? How many times? I, no no no, I renounced my Canadian citizen – don't mock me! I renounced my Canadian citizenship. I am not a fucking, I'm not gonna be suckered in, I'm not gonna be part of, I'm not gonna be suckered in like you idiots to this imperialistic, capitalistic, racist, whitewash, superiority-complex country –

DANDELION: Okay, calm down, relax –

SKIN: No no. Because you've asked me this before. Why don't you –

RATA: Okay.

DANDELION: Fine! I'm sorry! Just stop with the bad karma.

RATA: (*referring to SKIN*) Somebody shut her up –

DANDELION: God! Go take an anger management course or something.

SKIN: Fuck, man.

DANDELION: (*to ZAP, referring to marriage*) Why don't you do it?

ZAP: Really. They're really gonna believe two Latin American males are gonna get married.

DANDELION: What? You're too macho for that?

ZAP: Uh, I think it's illegal.

RATA: I'm not even gonna pretend I'm a fag.

SKIN: Shut up –

ZAP: Don't be such a homophobe, Rata.

SOMBRA: (*to RATA*) See? You're the only one who can marry him. Dandelion, you're saving this man's life. When he gets deported back to Guatemala –

DANDELION: Excuse me, but there's nothing going on in Guatemala any more. If there was, he could apply for refugee status and he'd get it, okay? He has to marry someone 'cause he knows he doesn't have a case for refugee status 'cause Guatemala's okay now. Why are you guys always trying to pull the wool over my eyes?

SKIN: Oh my God. Hold me back 'cause this chick is too ignorant. Hold me back – I mean like this tree-hugger actually thinks that 'cause the media says Guatemala's okay then Guatemala must be okay, oh gee –

SOMBRA: Haven't I told you the story about my *tío* Checho when he got deported back to Guatemala a couple of years ago? Three months. Three months he was back.

SKIN: Remember Uncle Checho? Remember her uncle Checho or do we need to remind you? 'Cause I can remind you. I'm very good at reminding people about these things. Okay: after Uncle Checho was deported from Canada back to Guatemala, he was placed in a jail. Okay? You know what a jail is?

DANDELION: Yes, I do.

SKIN: In Latin America? Okay. One year and a half. The man cannot walk straight any more. He walks with a limp. Every time the alarm clock goes off he talks to the alarm clock for an hour in the morning. He sings to himself, like, fucking military songs. Do you want that shit to happen to Rata? Do you want that to come down on your conscience?

DANDELION: Your uncle was a political activist; Rata's not. Why would he be arrested –

SKIN: Oh my God –

SOMBRA: Shhh. I'll explain. Rata left the country illegally, that's all that matters in their eyes. To them, that's enough "evidence" that he must have been in the underground, they'll arrest him for sure.

DANDELION: (*to RATA*) Why did you leave if you weren't involved in politics?

RATA: I had no money and no hope for the future. I wanted a new land.

SOMBRA: Come on, Dandelion, it'll be good for your karma if you marry him. Maybe your next life won't be shit if you sacrifice this time around.

Pause.

DANDELION: Okay. Fine. I'll do it.

RATA runs over to DANDELION, falls on his knees, and hugs her legs.

RATA: Thanks. Thanks.

DANDELION: Don't touch me! Get your hands off me! Gross!

There is a knock at the door, stage left.

SOMBRA: I'll get it.

The knocking gets more intense. SOMBRA opens the door to reveal JULIO.

JULIO: Hi. Is Rata here?

SOMBRA: Who are you?

JULIO: I'm a friend of his. (*walking into the room*) Hey, Rata!

SOMBRA: Rata, do you know this guy?

RATA: Yeah. He's my old buddy from Guatemala, he just arrived, I was gonna introduce you guys to him but then all this happened –

SOMBRA: Yeah, you look familiar –

RATA: We're working at the construction site – What's going on?

JULIO: It's good that you're here.

RATA: Julio, what's up?

JULIO: Immigration came for you.

RATA: What?

JULIO: Yeah, and –

SOMBRA: And you came here?

JULIO: Yeah, and –

SOMBRA: And you came here?

JULIO: Yeah, and you –

SOMBRA: Are you an idiot? They probably followed you, man. The secret police is probably standing right there, I knew that car was –

JULIO: Yeah, anyway, the idiotic boss said that yeah, that you have been working when they came, so –

RATA: Holy –

SOMBRA: Okay, you guys have to get out of here –

RATA: Holy holy holy –

SKIN: Yes.

ZAP: Fuck.

SOMBRA: (*to RATA and ZAP*) Get out of here. No. Go out the back. Go out the back. (*to JULIO*) Not you! Not you! They saw you come in and they have to see you come out.

JULIO: Okay.

SOMBRA: Umm ... go take a ferry to, like, Victoria or something.

RATA and ZAP exit through the back, and JULIO exits through the front. The three women are left.

SOMBRA: God that guy looks familiar –

DANDELION: The smell of this dress is making me wonky –

SKIN: Why? 'Cause we got it out of the dumpster?

SOMBRA: Shhh! Don't tell her that!

SKIN: What? I thought Granola likes recycling.

DANDELION: Oh my God! Did you even wash it?

SKIN: You're a tree-hugger, Granola, I thought you disagreed with detergent.

DANDELION jumps down from the chair.

DANDELION: (*pulling the dress off*) Not if it's phosphate-free, you idiot! There's probably rat piss on this fucking dress!

SOMBRA: Don't worry, we'll fix it. Make it look nice for the wedding.

DANDELION: I can't believe you talked me into this. I can't fuckin' believe I'm going to have to live with this guy for a whole year –

SKIN: Look upon it as a contribution to the *raza*, Granola.

DANDELION: My name is Dandelion.

SKIN: Whatever.

SOMBRA: No, really, Dandelion. Thanks. It's really nice of you to save Rata's life. Besides, you might start to like him, you know –

SKIN: You might end up doing the ol' shaky shaky –

DANDELION: Don't be disgusting.

SKIN: To think the fool never told us he walked here and never got no papers. Remember when Rolo and Pepo introduced him to us all? He looked so innocent, we all took pity on him, what with him being fresh off the boat and all, we took him on as a brother, and still he never confided –

SOMBRA: He's good at keeping his mouth shut about security matters. You'd never know it to look at him. He'd be a good revolutionary.

DANDELION: You guys, I don't know how I'm gonna tell my boyfriend about this –

SKIN: Who? That guy with the blond dreadlocks, Peruvian sweater, Guatemalan pants, and Tibetan beads? He plays a panpipe and –

DANDELION: His name is Josh McDougall and he's on the kind of journey you could never comprehend, okay?

SKIN: Well, whatever path the white guy's on, he could at least decide which culture he's gonna appropriate from, or if he's that desperate for a cultural identity, why doesn't he try his own roots?

DANDELION: He plays the bagpipes, okay?

SKIN: You have got to be kidding.

DANDELION: We're supposed to be going up to the interior to support a roadblock in a couple of weeks, I don't even know if I have time to marry Rata –

SKIN: Well, at least you weren't planning to go on some plastic boat trying to save the fuckin' whales 'cause then I would have had to –

SOMBRA: Dandelion, just stick with it, okay? It'll be good karma if you just marry Rata –

SKIN: Besides. We all have stuff to do. Like I'm giving a big fuckin' speech for the Student Union tomorrow first thing and I haven't even written it yet.

SOMBRA: Yeah. And I gotta get up first thing and wax apples.

SKIN: And if your boyfriend doesn't warm up to the idea, we'll just hold him hostage and cut off the dreadlocks one by one as I give him a lesson in Neo-colonialism 101. I'm good at educating white people about certain things, you know, it only takes a couple of minutes – or hey! If he's on this incomprehensible journey you talked about, we can send him to India to find himself, or do white people go to Tibet now? Which is in? As for me, when I lose myself I just go to the bathroom mirror and –

DANDELION: Why do you hate white people so much?

SKIN: Fuck. You just don't get it. I don't hate white people. I hate the concept of whiteness, white is not a skin colour, it's a state of mind, it's – how can I explain it to you? It's –

SOMBRA: I hope those guys are okay.

DANDELION: I'm gonna get going, you guys, this is too much. I need to chant.

SOMBRA: I got an old rosary of my mother's if you wanna use it.

SKIN: Sombra, she's not a Catholic, she's a liberal, remember?

SOMBRA: No! She's Jewish, but she can still use my rosary if she wants –

DANDELION: I'm a Buddhist.

SKIN: I didn't know you had your mom's rosary.

SOMBRA: Oh, yeah, I've kept it all these years. My mom was an atheist of course, but my grandma showed me the rosary from her First Communion, it's an antique –

DANDELION: I gotta go chant.

SOMBRA: (*looking out the window*) Dandelion, you gotta stay. If Immigration is after Rata then we gotta make this look like a real wedding. You know, if they show up here tonight and they see us three working on the wedding dress, then it all looks real. Just stick it out. Dandelion, Buddha will reward you.

SKIN: Hey, Sombra, let's see the rosary.

SOMBRA: Okay.

SOMBRA leaves the room.

SKIN: Hey. Thanks for marrying him. I know it ain't your thing. But thanks.

DANDELION: You're welcome.

SOMBRA re-enters with a rosary.

SOMBRA: Here it is. See? It's super old. Passed down for generations.

SKIN: Man, that kicks butt, man.

DANDELION: That's beautiful.

SOMBRA: It's all I have. This and a picture.

SKIN: Cool.

DANDELION: What about your dad?

SOMBRA: Just the memory. But when I go back to Guatemala maybe I'll find some old stuff of his at my grandma's place … I have the birthday card they gave me for my tenth birthday. That's the day they were taken away. On my birthday. As I was hitting the piñata my dad made for me. I always remember that. I even have a recurring dream about me hitting the piñata and opening my eyes and seeing the death squads taking my mom and dad away.

SOMBRA plays thoughtfully with the rosary. She puts it on.

Let's keep working on the dress.

SKIN: Okay, and I'll practice my "Rainbow Nation" speech on you guys.

DANDELION: Rainbow Nation?

SKIN: It's part of the Student Union at the college. It's the people of colour of the Student Union. We have our own space and I'm giving a big speech tomorrow. Let me practice on you guys while we work on the dress. Tell me if it's too harsh.

SOMBRA: Okay.

DANDELION and SOMBRA clear the chair and wedding dress as "Come Baby Come" by K7 begins to play. SKIN starts dancing like crazy. RAINBOW NATION STUDENT UNION MEMBERS dance behind her. The music stops and she addresses her speech to the audience and the RAINBOW NATION STUDENT UNION MEMBERS who sit around her.

SKIN: Welcome to the Rainbow fucking Nation.

Okay, a few years back, as a lot of you may or may not know, this room was given to us by the white, bleeding-heart liberal student body, okay? They said, "We want you, the people of colour, to have a place where you can feel free and open and safe to speak about issues on your mind." But then they had the audacity to name it for us. Rainbow Nation. Now, what kind of fucking name is

Rainbow Nation? Okay, I don't know about you, but when I think of a rainbow I think of harmony, peace, love ... I don't feel peaceful. I don't feel harmonious. And I sure as fuck don't feel love. I don't feel like I'm part of the multicultural mosaic when I'm surrounded by bleeding hearts who suffer from amnesia about their own country and hide behind a mask of political correctness and a fake fucking smile, "Hey, what's up?" I don't feel harmonious surrounded by people who speak the right jargon and yet you have no idea what they're really thinking, but you can sure as hell bet they're thinking, "Spic, go home." 'Cause I would rather have the clarity of a KKK member standing in front of my house burning a cross, on a horse with a white cloak and a white hood, so that I can see with my very eyes that he is the enemy and then I can say, "Okay, you're a racist, now get the fuck out of my life." And I shoot him. And it's self-defense. We are living in Vancouver. A place where white supremacists beat an old Sikh brother to death, where they chase Black brothers out of the Ivanhoe with baseball bats, where they beat the crap out of Filipino brothers in Squamish, where everywhere I look I'm portrayed as a fuckin' drug dealer 'cause I'm a Latino. Peace, harmony, love my ass.

So the first thing I wanted to ask you to do next Thursday, when you all get ballots to vote for who's gonna represent the Rainbow Nations to the Student Union, I want you to think Skin. And I want you to mark an X there. Why? The main reason, because the first thing on my agenda is change the name of these twenty cubic inches of room to – now I want you to brace yourselves, because a lot of research and study went into this name: Shades of Revolution. Now I know it's a really good name, but I wanna explain to you, hold the applause back, because I wanna explain to you exactly how I came to that name. First of all, shades. Why shades? Because we're all of colour here, but we're all of different colours. Shades. Shades that are threatening to them. All right? You, you're a little lighter than me, and you're a little darker than me, but we're all of colour. I don't know about you, but in my country, back in my country, I am not considered a person of colour. I step on this soil and I'm of colour. And revolution – and this is the beauty of the whole name – is because there's not one word in the English vocabulary that frightens and scares the white Canadian more than the word "revolution." 'Cause Shades of Revolution is the name that's gonna make the white Canadian person, or male, female – let's say man – shit his pants in fear.

So what I'm saying is that next Thursday, when you get the ballot, think of Skin. And repeat to yourselves those words: Shades of Revolution. (*beginning to snap her fingers and dance to the words*) Shades of Revolution –

"Crooklyn" by the Crooklyn Dodgers comes on as SKIN continues to dance to her own words.

Shades of Revolution, Shades of Revolution, Shades of Revolution, come on, oh Shades of Revolution ...

SKIN dances right offstage with her fellow RAINBOW NATION STUDENT UNION MEMBERS as they all dance and sing along to her words. The music fades out.

SCENE FOUR

"Sí I'm a Lowrider" by El Vez plays as lights come up on RATA. He is washing dishes at Ayayay Mexican restaurant.

The phone starts ringing. RATA doesn't know whether to answer it or not.

ZAP enters wearing a Mariachi outfit. He answers the phone.

ZAP: (*with a fake Spanish accent*) Hello and *buenas noches*. This is Ayayay Mexican restaurant at your service. Yes, sir. That's right. Authentic Mexican cuisine with authentic Mexican service. No, sir. Tamales are Salvadorean. We serve Mexican food. That's right. Of course we have burritos. Vegan? No sir, not vegan. Mexican. Okay sir. Yes, right in the heart of Commercial Drive. Open till late. *Buenas noches*, sir. (*taking off the Mariachi hat, losing the fake Spanish accent*) I'm gonna have to go out there soon to sing happy birthday with a fuckin' maraca. How's it all going back here?

RATA: Good. Other than the flood.

ZAP: The flood?

RATA: It took me a while to learn the mechanism of this dishwasher, but I've got it all under control now.

JULIO enters.

JULIO: Hey you guys, How's it all going?

RATA: Julio! I don't know if you should be here, man.

ZAP: Would you just relax, Rata? Everything's okay. (*to JULIO*) Come on in, man. Make yourself at home. Sit on this milk box.

JULIO: I just wanted to make sure you were okay, Rata.

RATA: Yeah, I'm okay. (*to ZAP*) Julio was my neighbour in Guatemala when I was growing up. Always let me play soccer with him and the bigger guys.

ZAP: Cool. You just got here?

JULIO: Two months ago.

ZAP: Well cool. Hang out with all of us, man. If you're a friend of Rata's you're a friend of ours.

RATA: Julio's more like family, right man?

JULIO: Absolutely. I used to walk Rata to school when he was small.

ZAP: More reason to welcome you into our group of friends. Family is family, man. Hey, Rata, bring him to our fundraiser on Saturday night –

RATA: Yeah, yeah … You're sure your boss is okay with me working under the table like this?

ZAP: Mariana? Are you kidding? She's my aunt. She's known me since I was born. She adores me. Don't worry about it.

RATA: What if –

ZAP: She will not give you away. She's with us, man. These boots are killing me. Come on, take a break. You've been at it for five straight hours. Sit down.

RATA: Yeah, but your aunt –

ZAP: She's gone for a while. Here. Sit on this milk box.

They both sit next to JULIO.

ZAP: (*to JULIO*) You need a job too, man? You know, straight cash, no papers?

JULIO: Oh no, man. Thanks for offering, though.

ZAP: Family's family man.

JULIO: No. I'm here with my papers. Rata got me work at the construction site till I get a steady job, but it's all above board. I got my work permit, and I'm waiting for my permanent papers so I can bring my wife and kids here –

ZAP: (*to RATA*) Why didn't you just do that, man?

RATA: I don't have a case, Zap.

ZAP: A case for what?

RATA: Refugee status. And I'm a man of principles. I don't like to lie about shit like that.

ZAP: (*to JULIO*) And you do have a case?

JULIO: Yeah. I do.

Pause.

ZAP: Harsh stuff at home?

JULIO: Yeah. Too traumatic to talk about.

ZAP: Sorry, man.

RATA: I really gotta thank you, man. Finding the priest, getting Dandelion to marry me, getting me this job, thanks, man.

ZAP: Shut up. So what's the story? How the fuck did you get away with being here for two whole years with no papers and never telling anyone? How'd they find out about you?

RATA: My old boss at the construction site must have told one of the supervisors and he must have given me away. I guess it had to happen sometime.

ZAP: So you never landed at Vancouver Airport?

RATA: No. I walked.

ZAP: From Guatemala?

RATA: Yup. Walked, swam, boiled my ass off on trucks, froze my ass off on freight trains.

ZAP: Scary shit, man.

JULIO: Rata always was crazy.

RATA: I've seen it all. (*to JULIO*) I can't believe you've joined me here, man.

ZAP: (*to RATA*) Harsh shit back home?

RATA: I saw a lot of harsh shit. The kind of stuff we can't even talk about. (*to JULIO*) I gotta admit I almost fell off my chair when you came here, man, as a refugee. I never for a million years would have thought you'd get involved in politics. Never ever. You were always so, so, I dunno, business-oriented –

JULIO: Let's not talk about the past. I want to suffer from amnesia.

RATA: Right. The past is too harsh.

ZAP: Don't worry, man. We'll make sure you don't get deported. Even if we have to go on a hunger strike, you won't get deported. Besides. The letter says you've got a month to get your shit together. No need to walk around like a criminal. No need to hide out. You've got nothing to hide. You're engaged to be married. Act happy. Make it look real. Go to parties. Click your heels together. If they think you've got nothing to hide – and you don't man, you don't – then everything will be okay.

JULIO: I'll be your best man.

RATA: I'm here now. I don't wanna go back.

JULIO: Do you feel Canadian?

RATA: I'm a man of the world.

ZAP: I wish I could feel like that.

RATA: You're Canadian, Zap. What are you talking about? You've got this land, this land's got you. You were raised here. Simple. You're Canadian. Clear as water.

ZAP: Yeah, right. Clear as fuckin' mud. I'm twenty years old and I still look at myself in the mirror every morning wondering who the hell I am. Am I Mexican? Am I Canadian? Am I just plain Latino? Am I Mexican Canadian? Am I Latino Canadian? Do I wanna –

RATA: What are you? Schizoid?

ZAP: No!

RATA: You're making me dizzy.

ZAP: It's called a cultural identity crisis, Rata –

JULIO: Man. And I thought I had problems 'cause I was in a concentration camp. Geez. Cultural identity crisis? Never heard of such a thing. I'm just plain old Guatemalan –

RATA: You and your gringo bullshit. You're just yourself. Just fuckin' be yourself.

ZAP: Be what? What?

RATA: I hate this whining. Just shut up and be.

ZAP: Yeah, but I don't know who to marry 'cause I don't know who I am.

RATA: What the hell are you talkin' about?

JULIO: Huh?

ZAP: I'm so mixed up I don't know if I wanna be with a white girl or a Latina girl –

RATA: You're really fucked up, man. Relax. You're only twenty. Date a lot of girls. Eventually you'll meet the one you wanna marry.

JULIO: Who cares where they're from –

ZAP: Yeah, but every time I'm with a chick all I can do is compare her to a Latina or a white girl. It's making me crazy. You guys don't get it 'cause you're only with Latinas. Let me give you this analogy. It's like white girls are like a bottle of chilled white wine. Goes down smooth. But they're cold. Latin girls are like red wine. Goes down hard and rough. But they're warm. Hot-blooded. Passionate – fuck. Forget about the girls. I'm so confused in myself. Maybe I should go to some cross-cultural support group or something –

JULIO: What's a support group?

RATA: Oh my God. You're more fucked up than I thought. Why don't you just go to a dating service, tell them what you're looking for, and take it from there. I mean if what you want is a girl, do that, man.

ZAP: I mean, like, I pray to get some clarity, but it just ain't –

JULIO: Go to a party, man, you, you wanna meet a girl –

RATA: Sure sure sure. Pray to San Judas. Tadeo, Guadalupe, Yemaya, Shango – spend your life praying, man, but if what you want is a girl and you ain't satisfied, go to a dating service.

ZAP: Are you serious? That's for, like, fuckin' losers –

JULIO: No offense, but if you're gonna talk about losers –

RATA: Look. Since you've done me all these favours, I'll figure this out for you. I'll find you a good dating service and –

ZAP: Naw –

RATA: I'll go with you. I'll do you the favour.

ZAP: You're gonna ask for a girl too?

RATA: No. I'm engaged, remember? I'll just accompany you. Come on. You want to find the right girl so badly, then get practical. Or you can continue praying. It's your choice, man. Remember. We're like family, man.

ZAP: So you'll come with me.

RATA: I'll take you by the hand.

ZAP: I'll think about it.

ZAP gets up, puts on his hat, grabs a maraca, and leaves the stage. RATA and JULIO look at each other and shake their heads.

JULIO: Lucky for us we didn't grow up here, man.

RATA: Take pity on them, Julio. It's not their fault they're so fucked up.

Rata gets up and continues washing dishes. Blackout.

SCENE FIVE

"Homies" by A Lighter Shade of Brown plays full blast. Lights come up on MÓNICA SONORA DINAMITA. She sits at a computer and talks on a cordless phone. The music cuts out. MÓNICA speaks with a thick Spanish accent.

MÓNICA: Mmm. Hmm-mmm. No, no. Charlie. Listen to me. Charlie. No. I am not going to call you Carlos *porque* Charlie, I know that you're not Latino. Charlie. Look. When you came to me and you asked me to find you a date, and you said, "Mónica, I need a date," I said, "Are you a lover?" and you said, "Yes," and I said, "Are you Latino?" and you said, "Yes." You lied to me, Charlie. No, Charlie, I am not going to call you – I know you have a tan. You can tell. You're starting to peel already. No, Charlie, look. When you came to me, you said, "I like Latina women." You told me the truth, but you did not tell me that you are a gringo. No. Charlie, no. Charlie, stop talking, because it's going in one ear and going out my nose. Charlie, no. Look, you know what I'm going to do, Charlie? And you should feel lucky that I don't get my brother and my uncles against you, I am going to blacklist you. Charlie, you are never going to date a Latina woman in the Greater Vancouver Area again. *Nunca más,* Charlie. Never again. You don't even understand what I'm saying, do you? No. And you know what else, Charlie? Because you lied to me, and you made a fool out of Mónica, I already blacklisted you from all other dating services.

DANDELION enters. MÓNICA gestures to her to sit down. DANDELION plays hackysack.

MÓNICA: Canadian, women on women, men on men, it doesn't matter. You will never date again. Charlie, look. I have another line. Look. No. We are not going to talk about this, okay? And you know what? There's a five-hundred-dollar penalty and I will take you to Small Claims Court – just – Charlie, look, I have to go. Look. *Chao. Adiós. Chao.*

DANDELION: Hey, Aunt.

MÓNICA: Oh, what a busy morning. Don't tell me you've finally come to your senses.

DANDELION: No Aunt, I already have a boyfriend –

MÓNICA: But I can find you a better one than that *gringuito*.

DANDELION: Aunt. No. I just came to see if you have a tiara I can borrow.

MÓNICA: You? My hippie niece is actually going to wear a tiara?

DANDELION: No Aunt. I mean yes. I'm going to wear a tiara, but not through a choice of my own.

MÓNICA: A costume party?

DANDELION: Sure. Yeah. A costume party.

MÓNICA: I think I can come up with something for you. I should have something at home.

DANDELION: Oh thanks. I knew you would.

MÓNICA: Now are you sure you don't want me to set you up with a nice Latin boy?

DANDELION: No, no. Aunt Mónica, the one time I let you try your tricks on me, you sent me on a date with this freak –

MÓNICA: Rocío, who was it? –

DANDELION: My name is Dandelion.

MÓNICA: Don't joke with me – José, right?

DANDELION: Uh, yeah. It was awful.

MÓNICA: He's a Latin man. You have to know how to treat them. They're toys. You have to know how to play a man like a toy, my little angel. You have to learn.

DANDELION: It was horrible! Remember? We went on a date to the Salsateca –

MÓNICA: And I got you the V.I.P. table –

DANDELION: Yeah, I know, reserved for –

MÓNICA: Latin Lovers Anonymous.

DANDELION: Remember what happened to me? The band started to play –

MÓNICA: Excellent band. The Salsonics, right?

DANDELION: He couldn't dance. You had gone on and on about what great dancers Latin men are and he couldn't even keep the most basic beat –

MÓNICA: Did you teach him everything that I've taught you?

DANDELION: Well –

MÓNICA: Did you move, did you move, did you move like a woman? The music was *conque conque conque conque* (*making music with her mouth and dancing*) *conque conque,* feel the music, woman. *Párate! Conque conque conque conque,* stand up! Move your hips – I remember when – move your hips! *Conque conque* –

DANDELION: I forgot how to dance, okay? It was the most embarrassing thing. I forgot how to dance.

MÓNICA: *Conque conque conque* – No!

DANDELION: I've been here too long to remember, besides, I don't go to salsa dances, I go to the Folk Festival –

MÓNICA: The Fuck Festival?! You forgot how to dance?

DANDELION: It was awful. I didn't know what the hell I was doing and my hands, you know –

MÓNICA: Rocío, it's all hips and boobs! *Conque conque conque* –

DANDELION: You could have at least looked in your database and found me a guy, you know, Latino, but that has been here as long as me, you know, forever, so he's kinda half and half, you know? That's what I'd asked for!

MÓNICA: What's wrong with José?

DANDELION: He was too Latino, man! He was fucking fresh off the boat.

MÓNICA: Don't swear at your aunt. I'll tell your mother. You can never be too Latino. Latino is in the soul.

DANDELION: He was too macho, okay? He ordered dinner for me.

MÓNICA: My father used to order dinner for me.

DANDELION: Your father?

MÓNICA: My father. *Qué te pasa?*

DANDELION: He was awful! He wouldn't let me go to the bathroom, and when I saw my cousin Luis there, he was all "who's that guy" and all this stuff –

MÓNICA: He's showing – he cares for you.

DANDELION: No. If that's the way he's gonna show it, I don't want it. You could have found me a guy that's not fresh off the boat, okay? This guy was fresh off the boat.

MÓNICA: Fresh off the boat? Oh, Rocío. Don't be racist!

DANDELION: Okay, okay. He was like ... he was too Latin.

MÓNICA: What do you mean, "too Latin?"

DANDELION: He was too Latino. I wanted someone not so Latino, you know, like me, I'm not so Latina, but, you know –

MÓNICA: That's your problem! You're not Latina enough. I taught you how to dance, how to dress – why are you wearing that horrible hippie outfit?

DANDELION: That's not the point, okay? Look at the – okay. You know. I did give him a chance because he looked like Ricky Martin and I figured –

MÓNICA: Like you asked –

DANDELION: You know, okay, so this guy looks like Ricky Martin, he's a bastard, but if I imagine hard enough, then maybe, just maybe ... so, you know we went back to his place, and things, you know, happened, or whatever –

MÓNICA: On the first date?

DANDELION: I was desperate, okay? Why do you think I let you put me up to it in the first place?

MÓNICA: There you go. If you look like you want respect you will get respect. I could tell your mother about this, you know.

DANDELION: She doesn't care – oh, you're so old-fashioned. See? That's what I'm saying. Okay. Anyways. He was in the bedroom, right, and I go to the bathroom and I say, oh, I'm going to get ready, or whatever, right, and I threw a condom, you know, a condom, on the bed, right? You know, I carry them in my pocket, right?

MÓNICA: *Claro.*

DANDELION: I go to the bathroom. I come out. Half-naked. And this man, who's fresh off the boat, doesn't know what the condom is. He opened it and started blowing it into a balloon. I swear to God this man did not know what a condom was. I'm sorry. He's so fresh off the boat he doesn't know what a condom is?

MÓNICA: No no. Of course he knows what a condom is, boat or no boat. I gave him pamphlets. I give all our men pamphlets. And I showed him how to use the condom with a banana –

DANDELION: Well, he kept saying something about skin to skin, or it's more natural –

MÓNICA: Ah no. He cannot put you in that position. Rocío, it's not about the boats. He knows all about condoms, he's just trying to fool you, all men are like that.

DANDELION: Anyway. Who cares. I have a boyfriend now anyway.

MÓNICA: Well, I will deal with him. I am going to blacklist him.

DANDELION: Aunt, it's okay. I'm sure there's lots of women who would love him. I gotta go. I'll stop by tomorrow to pick up the tiara.

DANDELION begins to exit as the phone rings.

MÓNICA: Latin Lovers Anonymous Dating Service, Mónica speaking. Teresita. Teresita, why are you crying? Teresita, I hope you are, last night you had a date with (*checking in computer*) Juanito. Juanito's a very good-looking man. Have you seen his ass? Very nice. *Pero,* Teresita, stop crying. I don't understand a word you say. What? One of my boys did not show up? No! Teresita! No! You cannot go to the dating service next door to mine. That one is Lesbian Lovers anonymous and I will tell your mother if you go there. I know where your mother lives. Okay. Look. I know – stop crying. Just – I know, stop crying, no. I'm going to tell you what I'm going to do to you, or for you (*going to her computer*), I am going to, on my database, I am going to blacklist him. Yes. He will never date a Latina here again. Yes, I know – oh! The other line is waiting! – I will find you another one, don't, *no te preocupes.* We'll go for a drink and – (*trying to put the phone down*) Yes, yes, yes, okay, yeah, yeah, yeah. Teresita, *mañana,* okay, hold on, okay, chao, chao, chao. Mua.

By this time, MÓNICA has her face flat against the desk, ear to the phone.

SCENE SIX

"On a Sunday Afternoon" by A Lighter Shade of Brown begins to play as the scene changes. MÓNICA exits with the chair, table, computer, and phone as DANDELION, ZAP, RATA, SKIN, and SOMBRA enter with drinks. The music morphs into a salsa that plays softly throughout the scene.

DANDELION: It looks good, doesn't it?

ZAP: Awesome.

SKIN: It looks really wicked.

RATA: So this is the Ukrainian Hall you guys talk about all the time.

SKIN: Yeah.

DANDELION: Yeah, when we were little we used to come here.

RATA: Hey, maybe we can have the wedding here –

DANDELION: Don't touch me! Gross.

SKIN: Yeah, the Ukrainian Hall. This brings back a lot of memories, man. This is where we used to always have our peñas, right, like when we were little. Like nine, ten years old. And all of us just gathered around, everyone paid a fee, an entrance fee, to come in. There were poets and your uncle used to –

DANDELION: Yeah, and Sombra's uncle used to sing. There used to be all these empanadas and pupusas and –

SKIN: Drinks.

RATA: But, did you do the same thing we're doing now, like sending the money –

SKIN: Yeah, it was for causes, like it was for the Mothers of the Disappeared in Argentina one time –

ZAP: And other political groups.

SKIN: Yeah. The FMLN in El Salvador.

ZAP: The Chilean Revolutionary Left Movement.

SKIN: The Sandinistas in Nicaragua.

SOMBRA: The URNG in Guatemala –

SKIN: I would like to propose a toast for all our hard work in getting this fundraiser together. Here's to us and here's to me for getting elected as the head of the newly named Shades of Revolution group of my Student Union at school.

ZAP, RATA, SOMBRA and DANDELION: (*together*) A toast! *¡Salud!*

They all drink.

RATA: What are you drinking?

DANDELION: Hemp ginger ale.

RATA: Have some wine –

DANDELION: And kill a million brain cells?

SKIN: And thanks, Dandelion and Sombra, for giving me some pointers on my speech that night. It kicked ass, man. I wish you all had been there for it. I blew them away, man. They were stoked.

DANDELION: Uh, you guys, I just wanna say that I'm really proud of us for doing this solidarity fundraiser and I was kind of wondering, you know, the thing where we're gonna send the money? I was wondering if maybe we could – like, we could give half to the Túpac Amaru Revolutionary Movement and the other half to my environmental group.

SOMBRA: We already talked about this last week –

DANDELION: 'Cause it's really important to me.

SKIN: What oppression does your environmental group suffer, man?

DANDELION: Um, okay, I don't know if you knew, but trees give us oxygen. Does that ring a bell?

SOMBRA: Dandelion, we're talking about human beings here –

DANDELION: I know that! I'm not saying –

SOMBRA: What good is clean air if there's no people around to breathe it?

DANDELION: I'm not saying –

SKIN: Exactly.

DANDELION: I'm not saying we have to give my group all the money, I'm just saying half and half.

SKIN: Did your blond-dreadlocked, bagpipe-playing boyfriend get you to bring this up?

RATA: Huh? That's okay. I'm not jealous.

DANDELION: Shut up. Excuse me, his name is Josh, and no, I have a mind of my own, you know.

RATA: I'm not giving money to bushes.

DANDELION: Pardon me, but trees are not bushes. And bushes are needed too.

SKIN: But, okay, but, Dandelion, we talked about this already.

DANDELION: Fine, can we do it for next time, then? If we're not gonna do it for this time –

SKIN: Well, no, next time we talked about having a fundraiser for my new Shades of Revolution –

ZAP: You've gotta understand. There's a reason why we're giving it to the Túpac Amaristas –

DANDELION: I know –

ZAP: She doesn't know –

RATA: Can you explain it to her –

SOMBRA: Don't explain it to her then –

DANDELION: I know. I'm not stupid. I know.

SKIN: That's okay, you guys, I'll remind her. I'm good at reminding people about these things. Just in case you didn't know, Granola, two years ago the Túpac Amaru Revolutionary Movement took a bunch of imperialist pigs hostage at the Japanese embassy in Lima, Peru – do you know where that is?

DANDELION: You are so insulting! I was born in Argentina, how can I not know where Peru is? Besides, me and Josh went backpacking in Machu Picchu –

SKIN: Good. Just checking. Anyway, these brave revolutionary comrades took a bunch of imperialistic pigs hostage and then they were blown away by the Peruvian military and nothing was ever said about them and their brave action again –

SOMBRA: Shhh! Don't talk so loud! For all we know the DJ's with the secret police and he set up microphones all over the place –

DANDELION: Can somebody shut Skin up, please –

SKIN: The point is that we have not forgotten their contribution to the struggle and we have decided to have this fundraiser and send the money to their families who lost –

DANDELION: Okay. I know. You don't have to repeat it to me, I'm not stupid, okay? I'm not an imbecile.

SKIN: Well, obviously you are because you're thinking of giving your money to trees. What the fuck is that?

DANDELION: I'm sorry, but I think it's a very good cause.

SKIN: The maximum we're gonna get is two hundred and fifty dollars. We're not gonna half it.

DANDELION: Okay fine. So next time.

ZAP: Okay, okay, okay. Dandelion's got a point. We should have a fundraiser someday for her group –

SOMBRA: Come on! Environmental groups get a lot of support already, we already talked about doing fundraisers for groups that really need the solidarity, like the Túpac Amaristas in Peru –

SKIN: Besides, if we're gonna have fundraisers to support local causes, it better be to support the homeless here or battered women or a solidarity fundraiser for the Indigenous activist Wolverine –

ZAP: Yeah! Wolverine!

RATA: Okay. I know you guys wanna do all these, uh, all these things you know, all these, uh, fundraisers and give money and all, and that's good, good causes, but one thing I don't understand is, how come you guys don't wanna keep any money for yourselves? I don't wanna be giving my money away.

SOMBRA: We're volunteering.

SKIN: What?

ZAP: It's volunteer.

RATA: Volunteer? Like, why am I doing this? Like, I didn't come all this way over here to, like, give my money away.

SKIN: It's out of the goodness of your heart, Rata.

RATA: I busted my ass to get up here. I don't wanna fucking – "Here: you know, help yourself. You know, I'm fucking dying here, but here."

ZAP: Rata, you're just spending a little bit of time toward the solidarity.

SKIN: Exactly. Doesn't that make you feel good inside, man?

RATA: No.

SKIN: It doesn't.

JULIO enters the hall.

SKIN: Come in, man.

JULIO: Is the party here?

SKIN: Yeah! You're the first person, so –

RATA: Julio! Good to see you here! Remember him you guys? My old neighbour from Guatemala –

SKIN and DANDELION: (*together*) Oh, yeah!

SKIN: Come on in, man. Make yourself at home.

The salsa tune gets louder.

JULIO: So, you are from ... are you from Guatemala?

SKIN: I'm from Chile.

JULIO: Oh! It's so good to be with Latinos again.

ZAP: Well, enjoy. Drink! Dance! It should be getting crowded anytime soon.

ZAP grabs SKIN and they dance.

JULIO: (*to SOMBRA*) Would you like to dance?

SOMBRA: Uh, yeah, sure, if you want.

JULIO and SOMBRA begin to dance.
RATA and DANDELION dance.

JULIO: So. Your name is?

SOMBRA: Uh, Gabriela.

JULIO: Gabriela?

SOMBRA: Yeah.

JULIO: Oh. That's a beautiful name. Where are you from?

SOMBRA: I'm from Guatemala too.

JULIO: From the capital?

SOMBRA: Yeah –

JULIO: I'm from zone six, same as Rata. What about yourself?

SOMBRA: Oh, I, I can't remember. Um, yeah.

JULIO: For how long have you been here?

SOMBRA: Oh, a long time. Like years.

JULIO: And you don't miss Guatemala?

SOMBRA: Uh, yeah, yeah, I miss it. Um, I think I've had too much to drink. I'm just gonna sit down. Thanks anyway.

JULIO: But, um, we might dance later –

SOMBRA: Yeah.

JULIO: If you want.

SOMBRA grabs SKIN and pulls her aside.

SKIN: What's going on, man?

SOMBRA: Um ...

SKIN: What's the matter with you?

SOMBRA: Um, you know Julio, Rata's friend from Guatemala, right?

SKIN: You look like you just saw a ghost. What's wrong with you?

SOMBRA: It's just ... I think, I think I recognize him.

SKIN: Did he hurt you?

SOMBRA: No! Shhh! Keep it down.

SKIN: Did he touch you?

SOMBRA: No.

SKIN: Do you like him?

SOMBRA: I'm being serious.

SKIN: So am I. What's wrong with you?

SOMBRA: I think I recognize him from Guatemala, okay?

SKIN: What, like an old family friend?

SOMBRA: No, I ... I could be wrong, okay?

SKIN: Spit it out, man!

SOMBRA: I think I recognize him from when they disappeared my parents, okay?

SKIN: Rata would never be friends with a torturer.

SOMBRA: You are so naive. You think that torturers walk around with signs on their backs or something? They have families and wives and friends, you know.

SKIN: But he doesn't even look like one –

SOMBRA: Do you know how many people come here and they say they're refugees and they're fucking torturers? I think I'm gonna go, man.

SKIN: No! You're not gonna go. I'm gonna call Rolo and Pepo, man.

SOMBRA: No, no. I could be wrong, okay?

SKIN: No, we're gonna get this fucking – Rolo and Pepo pack all the time, man.

SOMBRA: I know, they're crazy, no. Look, I'm not gonna do the same thing to them that they did to us.

ZAP approaches.

SKIN: She thinks that asshole is a torturer.

SOMBRA: Shut up. Keep it down.

ZAP: What?

SKIN: She thinks that asshole is one of the guys that showed up at her house and took her parents away in Guatemala.

ZAP: What?

SKIN: Don't stand there like a numbskull. Do something!

ZAP: What?

SOMBRA: Shut up, you guys. Act normal. He's looking at us. Just act normal. These people are dangerous.

SKIN: I say let's call Rolo and Pepo –

SOMBRA: Man, you guys are stupid. Do you know how dangerous these people are? Besides, I don't want to be just like them.

RATA comes over.

RATA: What are you guys doing? Having a meeting? I know you take your politics very seriously, but don't you know this is a party, as in p-a-r-t-y –

SOMBRA: Just go back there. He's noticing something's up –

RATA: Who?

DANDELION comes over.

DANDELION: I'm gonna kill Josh. He was supposed to be here half an hour ago and – hey, can I use your cellphone?

RATA: Uh, honey, I'm sorry to say I ran out of batteries –

DANDELION: Don't call me – but I just saw you using it –

RATA: I know. And the stupid thing ran out of batteries in the middle of my call. Hey my flower, since you wanna raise money for your group I was thinking that we could have the wedding right here and make a fundraiser out of it, you know give the proceeds to the bushes – I'm dead serious, I swear I'm not making fun –

SKIN: Hey! Hand over the cell! I'll call Rolo and Pepo –

SOMBRA: Skin, I will kill you if you call those guys –

RATA: What? You have a crush on Rolo and Pepo –

JULIO comes over.

JULIO: I have to get going. I just got a job working the graveyard shift at the sugar refinery, so I gotta head out –

RATA: Well, thanks for coming, man, and partying with my friends. I'll walk you out, let me just go to the can first.

RATA exits.

JULIO: Well, this was a wonderful time. It's so good to be with Latinos again. Rata has a great group of friends. Who are you raising funds for?

ZAP: Uh, her environmental group. We're raising funds for the environment. You know –

SKIN: Trees.

DANDELION: And bushes.

ZAP: They give us oxygen you know, and that damned ozone layer –

SKIN: (*to DANDELION*) Do you ride a bike? You should really ride a bike 'cause cars are the worst, man.

JULIO: Wonderful. I have to go to work now. I'll come to your fundraisers again. (*to SOMBRA*) Thank you for the lovely dance. It's been a long time since I've been with my compatriots. You've brought back beautiful memories of home. Goodbye.

Pause. JULIO leaves.

SKIN: Holy shit. Good cover-up, Zap. What are we gonna do now?

DANDELION: Are you guys ripped on some weird drug or what?

SKIN: Julio is one of the guys who raided Sombra's house in Guatemala and disappeared her parents. She recognized him when they were dancing –

DANDELION: Holy shit. Are you okay, Sombra?

ZAP: Let's call the cops.

SOMBRA: No!

ZAP: Sombra, I know you hate cops but in some cases they're okay –

SOMBRA: You have no idea how dangerous these guys are. Calling the cops would mean –

SKIN: Okay. She's right. Let's think of a plan of action. You know, tactics for the strategy.

SOMBRA: Oh God. It's him. I can't believe he's here.

ACT TWO

SCENE ONE

Lights up on the VIRGIN GUADALUPE, patron saint of Mexico as "Beija-Flor" by Timbalada plays.

The VIRGIN stands upstage in stillness for the first few bars of the song. Then she dances in a circle, swaying her hips.

ZAP enters, holding a rosary, and kneels. The VIRGIN dances a little while longer, and goes still. ZAP crosses himself.

ZAP: Hi, Virgin. It's me, Zap. Just came from another date. I had nowhere else to go. This time it was Becky. You know, your typical suburban *Brady Bunch*–meets–*Melrose Place* white girl, you know. Run-of-the-mill. Pretty. Cute. She was cute, she was polite. We met in poli-sci class. She was really nice, but all she wanted the whole night was for me to speak in Spanish, or at least, you know, do my best Spanish accent in English. Run her hands through my sparsely balding chest. You know, all she wanted was to talk about Che Guevara and the revolution.

I don't know about white girls, Virgin. I mean, in a way it's good. You don't have to call them for weeks on end. You call up and they're at it, hey, yeah, let's go. With a Latin girl, you have to call her every day, thrice a day, or it's over. You know, it's over. And when it comes to stuff like sex, with a white girl all I have to do is clean the sheets afterward and it's okay. She's happy. A little pillow talk and she's happy. Latin girls? Let's just say sex is basically the signing of the prenups. White women exude this unintentional coldness. I'm not sure if you can understand what I'm talking about. I mean you have sex and stuff and afterward it's just like, "Hi, yeah, how's it going." Latin girls? They're like leeches. But they have this intangible, indescribable warmth that you just can't feel with white girls.

Forget about the girls, Virgin. What am I? Who am I? This is a nightmare.

The VIRGIN shares a smile and roll of the eyes with the audience.

ZAP and the VIRGIN exit.

SCENE TWO

RATA and SOMBRA enter with milk boxes on which they sit. They are in the kitchen of Ayayay Mexican restaurant.

RATA: Are you absolutely sure that it's him, Sombra?

SOMBRA: One hundred percent. I had a feeling about him that night he showed up at the house, but when I danced with him at the fundraiser I knew. I totally knew.

RATA: You know, Sombra, that was a really long time ago and you were really small –

SOMBRA: I may have been really small, Rata, but there are certain things that I remember with precision.

RATA: There's just no way. Julio was one of us. He took care of me in the neighbourhood, and when I had to get away, he even gave me some money –

SOMBRA: So what? These men lead double lives –

RATA: But he married Francisca, his high-school sweetheart, and he's a great father to his two little kids –

SOMBRA: Oh my God, Rata. So what? He can torture people and still love his family! Don't you know that?

RATA: I just can't believe –

SOMBRA: I'm sorry, Rata. I know he's your friend but –

RATA: What am I going to say when I see him next?

SOMBRA: I don't know, Rata. That's your call.

RATA: You are one hundred percent sure –

SOMBRA: It was my tenth birthday, Rata, and I will never forget it …

The lights change as RATA and SOMBRA exit. A piñata drops into view and the sounds of a child's birthday party can be heard. A slide of a birthday card proclaiming "Happy Tenth Birthday, Gabriela! We love you, Mami and Papi" appears on the screen.

SOMBRA enters as a ten-year-old girl, dressed in a party dress. She is being escorted by her father. SOMBRA has a blindfold on and is holding a broom. Her father escorts her to the piñata, laughing, and she begins to hit the piñata as her parents look on, screaming, laughing, and clapping.

The sound of the broom hitting the piñata slowly transforms into the sound of a whip hitting a body. The screams turn into sounds of pain.

JULIO and two death-squad members enter. They are armed. They grab Sombra's parents and begin to take them away. SOMBRA continues hitting the piñata, unaware of what is going on. The piñata finally breaks open. Sand falls from it.

SOMBRA removes her blindfold to see her parents being taken away. She has eye contact with JULIO. They look at each other.

Blackout.

SCENE THREE

"Homies" by A Lighter Shade of Brown plays. Lights come up on MÓNICA. She talks on her cordless phone at her desk.

MÓNICA: Latin Lovers Anonymous Dating Service, Mónica speaking. Oh! You are interested in – okay. Well, how did you hear about us? Oh, she's a very good friend. I know. She's amazing. Okay, so let me start, you know, I am going to tell you a little about Latin Lovers. My name is Mónica Sonora Dinamita and, well, I started here with my ex-husband ten years ago, but we're still very good friends. Um, let me see, I knew there was a market for Latinos who cannot find Latinos like them here in Canada. So I opened up a place, you come to me, and for fifty dollars a month, you can be on our list and you will be on at least four dates a month. Yes. Yes. And we have a whole roster of people that you can take a look at. Very beautiful women. If you like men, we have that too. Okay. Perfecto. And I have to ask you two very important questions before we commence your application, yes? Eh, *la primera pregunta,* the first question is, um, are you Latin? Good. And the second question is, are you a lover? Aha. Very good. So, we will commence with the application –

ZAP and RATA enter. ZAP looks very uncomfortable.

MÓNICA: *(into the phone)* Uh, yes, just one second *(gesturing to RATA and ZAP to sit down and continuing to talk on the phone)* We'll take your picture, unless you have an eight-by-ten. Yes. Okay. Just one second. *(to RATA and ZAP)* Sit down. *(back into the phone)* Okay. And, why don't we do this? I take your number, yes? And I call you and we make an appointment to see each other, okay? And then we will dance, we will sing, we will drink.

Yes. Mónica. Mónica Sonora Dinamita. Okay. Thank you. Okay, perfecto. Okay. Chao. Mua. Chao.

She hangs up the phone.

Yes? What are you doing here? What do you want?

ZAP: Uh, I'm here, to get, uh, like, a date.

RATA: He wants a date.

MÓNICA: Ah, you want a date. I'm sorry, I'm sorry. Uhh. Ay, it's been a busy morning. Have a seat. Have a seat. Ah! I'm sorry. Uh, two questions: Are you Latin?

ZAP: Yes.

MÓNICA: And, are you a lover?

ZAP: Aspiring.

MÓNICA: Aspiring? Potential. Very good. Okay. So we will open up a file. Okay. Now. Why are you looking at me like that? What is your name?

ZAP: Zap.

MÓNICA: Sap? Like from a tree?

ZAP: No, like Zapata. Emiliano Zapata. Chiapas. Mexico. *Resistencia.*

MÓNICA: Who?

ZAP: Chiapas. The uprising in Mexico. Zapatistas. Zap. For short. Me.

RATA: He wants a date.

MÓNICA: What about you?

RATA: I'm engaged to be married. I'm just accompanying him.

MÓNICA: Oh! Congratulations! Okay, so Sap. What are you looking for in a woman?

RATA: From what I can understand, he wants somebody like him. He wants a girl who is half Latina and half Canadian. You know. Not fresh off the boat. And not white either. Like him. Someone who grew up here. Also, someone political. You see, he thinks he's the reincarnation of Che Guevara or something, so –

MÓNICA: Uh-huh. This generation is so complicated. Let me think. I've got the perfect person for you.

ZAP: Really?

MÓNICA: Oh, yes. Trust me. I've been matchmaking displaced Latinos for ten years.

"Mentirosa" by Mellow Man Ace comes on. ZAP and RATA continue to talk to MÓNICA as she looks into her computer. ZAP pays the fee. They all shake hands, and the three of them exit. The music cuts out.

SCENE FOUR

SOMBRA, ZAP, SKIN, RATA, and DANDELION enter. JULIO is upstage, locking up a door to the sugar refinery, back to the audience. It is very early morning. The group surrounds him. SOMBRA stands right by him. JULIO turns around and sees the group.

JULIO: Oh! Hello! What a nice surprise to see you all here!

SOMBRA holds a picture up to JULIO's face.

SOMBRA: Where are they?

JULIO: I don't know what you're talking about.

DANDELION, SKIN, ZAP, and RATA group around SOMBRA and JULIO.

SOMBRA: Look at the picture. Don't tell me you don't recognize them. I recognize you. Where are they?

JULIO: (*to RATA*) What is this? A joke?

SOMBRA: Where are they?

Lights change as all characters except JULIO freeze. He delivers his monologue to the audience.

JULIO: Tonight, you are having a banquet. Yes. A fried tortilla. Some cold rice and beans. You're lucky I didn't give these leftovers to the dogs. This food will be good for you. You will like it. We need you here for a few more days. I know that you wonder what makes me do this to you. What do I think about this place and what's going on here. To tell you the truth, not everything has to do with politics. At the beginning, yes. I am a good soldier. A proud officer.

I felt quite proud when the government gave me the task of getting rid of the scum of society. You. Terrorists. Communists. Lunatics. However, now it's a little bit more than that. This has become my pride. I enjoy every single second of it. This is no longer about whether I will be able to get the information out of you. Your movement is going to disappear. We are winning. We will win. No doubt about that. This is about whether at the end of every session you will feel ashamed. Defeated.

Would you believe that every morning I look forward to seeing you? I like it from the time I enter the room. (*starting to walk around*) I know. You are listening to my shoes. I like to walk around. You are trying to guess whether it's me, or the person that's just taking care of you, just to see if you are okay. I like to see the expressions on your face. Expressions of fear. Do you know that sometimes I start to move the tray, the metallic tray, on purpose? You are listening. You think that I am preparing my tools for another one of our sessions.

What I enjoy the most is when you are about to betray yourself. When you are about to give up. Your lips start to shiver. You swallow saliva. You close your eyes. And you do whatever I tell you. That's the moment of victory for me. I was frightened by the resistance that you and some of your friends put up. It seemed unbelievable. But time, practice, and experience have taught me that every single one of you has a breaking point. You poor soul. You are starting to play the role of the hero. And the things that you are doing are exciting me more. I'm more interested in you. So the next day I can come and try something new. A new trick.

Yes, friend. I know about you. More than you would like me to know. You know that the only hope you have now is that I won't be able to forget you. That when I leave the room your screams will be in my ears. That when I go home and take my kids in my arms and give them a hug, I'll be remembering your kids, that they'll be asking for you. To tell you the truth, that doesn't happen. In a few weeks, I will forget your face, your name, what you did, you will just be one of the others. So don't start to dream on. Soon enough, you will be nothing and you will never make it into the history books. You never existed.

Lights go back to normal, as the other characters come back to life. We're back at the sugar refinery.

You want to know the truth? There were so many. They might be in a ditch, a river, or who knows where.

RATA: No. Tell me it's not the truth, Julio. Tell me.

JULIO: They were terrorists, Rata. You are so fucking naive. Who do you think saved Guatemala from communism? I did. People like me. We did the dirty work for you, Rata, so you could live in peace –

RATA: Holy fuck. You. You're a torturer. I –

SOMBRA: And you think you can walk among us, claiming to be a refugee? Well, I am here to tell you that I offer you no impunity.

JULIO tries to get past the group, grabbing the picture from SOMBRA's hand and throwing it to the ground aggressively.

SOMBRA: Don't!

JULIO starts to run. He runs in slow motion, downstage.

SOMBRA: You have to pay for what you've done.

RATA: Julio!

SOMBRA: Come back here.

DANDELION, SKIN, ZAP, SOMBRA, and RATA chase JULIO. They all run in slow motion, downstage, JULIO in the lead. They finally catch up to him, and in slow motion bring him down to the ground, upstage.

"Matador" by Los Fabulosos Cadillacs begins to play full blast. Slides of Sombra's parents come up: Sombra's parents kissing, dancing, holding Sombra in their laps. If possible, use pictures of real disappeared people.

The group begins to dance in a circle around JULIO, who is on the floor. They beat him in slow motion. They do the Zapateo from the Chilean cueca *dance as SOMBRA moves downstage and dances a solo version of the Chilean* cueca*. Eventually, everyone dances away from JULIO, and exits as the music stops, leaving JULIO crumpled in a fetal position on the floor.*

SOMBRA stays on, looking down at JULIO. She directs her monologue at him and slowly raises her head, talking to the audience.

SOMBRA: I hate you. I can't even describe how I hate you. I hate you more for making me hate so much. You're disgusting. I'm not even gonna try to understand what you are, you don't deserve that much thought.

You have taken everything away from me. My mom and dad, my childhood, my *familia,* my country, but you will never be able to take away my humanity. That's the only thing I have left. You disappeared my parents, but they left me something. They left me my humanity. What have you left your children?

My parents may never make it into the history books, but you will. The whole world will know what you've done. 'Cause I remember. And my children will remember. And I know you'll remember. You have to.

You made such a big mistake. If what you wanted was to destroy the cause and the desire for people to live better, you should have killed me. You should have killed us all. 'Cause I have my memory, I have my humanity, but not you. So in the end, we win.

Lights out.

SCENE FIVE

Restaurant music begins to play in dim light. A table and two chairs are brought on as slides from the Love and Rockets *comic book appear on the screen.*

Lights come up on SKIN, all dressed up, sitting at the table. She is very nervous. She looks at her watch. She looks around.

RATA and ZAP enter. ZAP is carrying a single red rose. He is dressed up. They see SKIN from behind.

RATA: Okay. That must be her. You ready?

ZAP: Oh shit, man. This is crazy. Maybe we should just forget the whole –

RATA: (*pushing ZAP back into the restaurant*) Be a man. The lady's here. Grab some balls and go up to her and just give her the rose. Be polite. Don't swear when you talk. And don't start talking to her about politics right away. When in doubt about what to say, just recite poetry. You know, Pablo Neruda's twenty poems of love or something. Come on.

ZAP: Well, what are you gonna do?

RATA: I'll hang around. I'm here for you man. Now just go.

ZAP: Oh fuck. I can't believe you talked me into this.

RATA: (*pushing ZAP*) Be like a Latino, man. Suave. Confident. You got nothing to worry about. Just go.

RATA arranges ZAP's hair and clothes. He sprays cologne on him.

RATA: I'm here for you, man. Get over there.

ZAP crosses himself and starts heading toward the table. RATA hangs around upstage looking out of place, talking on his cellphone.

ZAP: (*approaching SKIN*) Excuse me, Miss, you must be here to meet me –

SKIN: (*turning around*) Oh yes – (*leaping to her feet*) Holy fuck! What are you doing here you idiot?!

ZAP and RATA: (*together*) Skin!

SKIN: What the?

RATA: I'm just accompanying him, giving him some balls –

ZAP: Don't tell me that you went to that Mónica Sonora Dinamita chick –

SKIN: Oh fuck.

ZAP: You, hardcore Skin, actually went to Latin Lovers –

SKIN: Oh, shut up. Look who's talking.

RATA: Jesus Christ. I go out of my way to get this guy a date and all along you could have been –

SKIN: Whoa! Hold it right, there, Mr. Lowrider Limo –

RATA: Mónica's right, man. You two are perfect for each other. Well, I'm off! See ya! Have a hot night!

RATA leaves. ZAP and SKIN are left standing alone in the restaurant, looking sheepishly at each other.

ZAP: I can't believe that you would go to that dating service –

SKIN: You say one word about this to the others and I will –

ZAP: I didn't know you were that desperate –

SKIN: It's a time thing, man. I don't have time to go look for guys so I got someone else to do it for me, okay? What the fuck is wrong with that?

ZAP: Oh nothing. Nothing.

Pause.

Well, as long as we're here, you wanna sit down?

SKIN: Oh sure, why not.

They both sit down.

ZAP: (*passing her the rose*) This was meant for ... you ... I guess.

SKIN: Thanks. It's very nice. Um, romantic, yeah.

ZAP: You look really nice. I've never seen you dressed like this before –

SKIN: Well, it's a date. This is how people dress for dates.

ZAP: So I guess we're on a date.

SKIN: Guess so ... You look nice, too.

ZAP: You think so? Rata chose my outfit.

SKIN: Rata? Rata actually has some taste?

ZAP: Did Mónica tell you I was perfect for you?

SKIN: Yup.

ZAP: That's what she told me about you.

SKIN: What'd you ask for?

ZAP: Someone like me. Latina, but not fresh off the boat. Raised here. Political.

SKIN: Kinda like what I asked for.

Pause.

ZAP: When we were twelve I had a crush on you, but I was too scared to –

SKIN: Me too.

ZAP: No way.

SKIN: Totally. I used to doodle hearts in my grade-seven notebook.

ZAP: Oh my God. I cannot imagine you, hardcore Skin, actually doodling hearts in your notebook –

SKIN: What's your fuckin' point?

ZAP: Oh, don't get me wrong. I like your hardness. It's a real turn-on – I mean, sorry, I don't mean sexually – I mean it's what I love about you.

SKIN: You don't think I'm too harsh?

ZAP: I think you're perfect.

SKIN: Most guys are terrified of me.

ZAP: They just don't know how to deal with a real woman.

SKIN: I can't believe this. I feel like when I was twelve right now. And I had the biggest crush on you. But it's more than that. I don't feel at home here. And there's no place like home. That Dorothy bitch was right, man. There is no place like home. And I don't feel at home here. I just don't. But I feel at home with you. I feel at home with you babe. Yeah.

ZAP: Me too.

"Fever" by El Vez begins to play. ZAP and SKIN stare at each other nervously. They giggle. ZAP takes SKIN's hand and slowly gets her on her feet. They giggle. They very awkwardly begin to slow dance, until they are in a full embrace. They giggle. They break into laughter. They kiss. A slide of a child's drawing of a heart appears in the screen. They keep dancing.

SCENE SIX

DANDELION, RATA, and SOMBRA enter. DANDELION is in her wedding dress. RATA is dressed to the nines. SOMBRA is also dressed up. RATA is talking on his cellphone.

RATA: Yeah! I'm still getting the lowrider limo! Yeah! Me and my wife-to-be are going on our honeymoon in it –

DANDELION: This is a wedding for the papers, remember?

SOMBRA: (*to ZAP and SKIN, who are still dancing and kissing*) Hey! You guys! It's their wedding, not yours! Break it up – we gotta get organized!

The music fades out as ZAP and SKIN disengage.

ZAP: Organize what? Everything's done!

RATA: (*into the cellphone*) Lowrider –

SKIN: (*grabbing the cellphone*) I think he must suffer from some mental illness –

RATA: Don't –

SKIN: (*examining the cellphone*) Oh my God! Oh my God, you guys, this is a fake phone! It's a toy cellphone!

RATA: Aw fuck.

SOMBRA: Get outta here. Oh my God. (*talking into the cellphone, mimicking RATA*) "Lowrider limo" –

RATA: Okay okay okay. Real ones are expensive, okay? So what? It's just a toy –

SKIN: That's it, man. You need help.

RATA: When you're in the North, you act like it. You get gadgets.

SOMBRA: You are too much, man.

DANDELION: (*laughing*) I think you're hilarious!

RATA: Why thank you. Hey Dandelion, you know how these two went out looking for someone and never even realized that the right person was right under their nose, well maybe, just maybe, that will happen to us –

DANDELION: You fucking wish –

SOMBRA: She has a boyfriend, remember?

SKIN: Hey, yeah! Is Mr. Dreadlocks-in-a-kilt coming or what?

RATA: Her fucking boyfriend at our wedding? Do I look like that much of an idiot to you?

DANDELION: He broke up with me, okay?

RATA: What?

DANDELION: (*to RATA*) All thanks to you!

RATA: You're more than welcome.

ZAP: He broke up with you?

SKIN: I thought white guys weren't possessive.

DANDELION: He said he met this chick at the Chrétien rally at the Hyatt –

RATA: Don't worry, babe. I'll console you.

DANDELION laughs.

SOMBRA: Don't worry about it, Dandelion. There's millions of guys out there.

RATA: Like me.

DANDELION: You never stop, do you?

RATA: I love your name, it's so plantlike.

DANDELION: Well I have to admit I love your name too. It's so rodent-like.

SOMBRA: Okay, so everything's set. People should be arriving soon. Father Joseph will be here any minute –

RATA: You got the donation box set up for the bushes and whales?

DANDELION: It's not for the bushes or whales. It's for my environmental group –

RATA: I know, Dandelion.

SOMBRA: Yeah, it's all set up.

DANDELION: Thanks for doing that, you guys.

RATA: Hey! It was my idea!

SOMBRA: (*pulling out camera*) Okay! Let's take a few pictures before the priest gets here! Dandelion and Rata, you go there. Good. Skin, you're the best woman, stand by Dandelion, and Zap, you're the best man, so stand by Rata. Go!

She snaps the picture.

Beautiful! Now, one of just the bride and groom. Excellent!

She snaps the picture.

Great. Now one of the best man and the best woman. Gorgeous.

She snaps the picture.

SKIN: Okay. Now one of you, Sombra.

SOMBRA: No way, man. I don't do pictures – Actually, yeah, take a picture of the new me.

SKIN snaps a picture of SOMBRA. The moment is held and highlighted with lighting and the sound of a shutter. SOMBRA has gone through a huge transformation, having confronted JULIO.

ZAP: I can't believe we pulled this thing off. You and Dandelion getting married at the Ukrainian Hall. A day before you're supposed to get deported.

RATA: I won't believe it until the papers are signed. You got the rings?

ZAP: Right here, man.

FATHER JOSEPH enters.

FATHER JOSEPH: (*with a heavy Irish brogue*) Hello, Zap!

ZAP: Hey, Father Joseph! You're here! Thanks for coming! Hey you guys, this is Father Joseph! This here's the bride and groom.

FATHER JOSEPH: What a lovely lass! You're a lucky man.

RATA: (*not understanding a single word of the Irish accent*) Huh?

SOMBRA: Let's start the ceremony! Remember we wanna get it done before people come for the fundraiser. Then we can dance and talk and stuff.

FATHER JOSEPH: All right. I've got the papers here. I need the bride and groom to stand right here.

FATHER JOSEPH moves upstage, as RATA and DANDELION face him.

FATHER JOSEPH: Who are the witnesses?

SKIN and ZAP: (*together*) We are.

FATHER JOSEPH: Good. Stand right there.

ZAP and SKIN stand on either side of DANDELION and RATA.

FATHER JOSEPH: Are we expecting anyone else at this ceremony?

SOMBRA: I sure as hell hope not.

FATHER JOSEPH: A small wedding. The more intimate, the better.

RATA: (*to DANDELION*) I can't understand a word he says –

DANDELION: Shhh. He's Irish, I think.

RATA: Fresh off the boat or what?

DANDELION: Ssshhh.

FATHER JOSEPH: All right. You have the rings?

SKIN and ZAP nod.

FATHER JOSEPH: Good. Here we go ... Do you, Raul Sandoval, take this woman to be the wife of your days?

RATA: Huh?

DANDELION: Just say "I do."

RATA: I do.

FATHER JOSEPH: Do you, Rocío Bernstein, take this man to be the husband of your days?

DANDELION: I do.

FATHER JOSEPH: Place the rings on each other's fingers.

RATA: What did he say?

DANDELION: Ssshhh.

SKIN and ZAP pass the rings. DANDELION and RATA place the rings on each other's fingers.

FATHER JOSEPH: I now pronounce you husband and wife.

Everyone cheers. DANDELION and RATA sign the marriage certificate. SOMBRA snaps a picture.

FATHER JOSEPH: You may kiss the bride.

RATA: Huh?

DANDELION laughs. She grabs RATA and plants a kiss on him. SOMBRA snaps a picture. Everyone cheers. FATHER JOSEPH exits.

SOMBRA: *¡QUE VIVAN LOS NOVIOS!*

ALL: (*together*) *¡Que vivan!*

SOMBRA: *¡Viva la raza!*

ALL: (*together*) *¡Que viva la raza!*

"La Raza" by Kid Frost begins to play.

RATA: (*into his fake cellphone*) James, bring the limo to the front and if you're a good *muchacho*, I'll let you feel my fuzzy dice. (*to DANDELION*) Let's dance, baby! –

DANDELION: Yeah.

RATA: Everyone dance! Dance! Dance!

The actor who played FATHER JOSEPH, JULIO, and other characters enters in his neutral costume.

All the actors become The Latino Theatre Group members again and begin to dance to "La Raza."

THE ACTOR WHO PLAYED SKIN: (*rap-like, to the others and the audience*) *¿Que pasa* with *la raza,* eh?

THE ACTOR WHO PLAYED DANDELION: (*to the others and the audience*) *¿Que pasa* with *la raza,* eh?

THE ACTOR WHO PLAYED ZAP: (*to the others and the audience*) *¿Que pasa* with *la raza,* eh?

THE ACTOR WHO PLAYED SOMBRA: (*to the others and the audience*) *¿Que pasa* with *la raza,* eh?

THE ACTOR WHO PLAYED JULIO: (*to the others and the audience*) *¿Que pasa* with *la raza,* eh?

THE ACTOR WHO PLAYED RATA: (*to the others and the audience*) *¿Que pasa* with *la raza,* eh?

ALL: (*to the audience*) *¿Que pasa* with *la raza,* eh?

The actors continue dancing as a slide appears. The slide says, "The borders have blurred, North is down and South is up: Welcome to the Americas." That slide dissolves into another that says, "The end, and Viva la raza."

ACKNOWLEDGMENTS

I would like to thank the Canada Council for the Arts for their support over the last twenty-five years. Without their funding through individual writing grants, travel grants, and project grants, I would not have been able to work as a theatre artist. Their contribution to the arts in this country cannot be overstated. I would also like to thank the British Columbia Arts Council for their support over the last twenty-five years, as well as the City of Vancouver. Public funding for the arts is what makes the arts possible.

I would like to thank my alma mater, Studio 58, for the best training there is, and for their unwavering support since 1990.

I would like to thank Guillermo Verdecchia, colleague, friend, and mentor, who changed everything for me when I went to watch his seminal work, *Fronteras Americanas*. His superlative dramaturgy and direction of *Chile Con Carne* is what has made that play an ongoing success, twenty-three years after it first premiered at the now-defunct Station Street Arts Centre in Vancouver.

I would like to thank Headlines Theatre Company (later Theatre for Living) for providing all of the support needed to start the Latino Theatre Group (which ran from 1994 until 2002) under their umbrella.

I would like to thank Augusto Boal and his Centre for Theatre of the Oppressed in Rio de Janeiro, Brazil, for the inspiration and the training, as well as Victoria's Puente Theatre, and Headlines Theatre for additional training in the form.

I would like to thank the Firehall Arts Centre in Vancouver for co-producing *¿QUE PASA with LA RAZA, eh?* and for being one of many homes for the Latino Theatre Group. Many thanks to the Playwrights' Theatre Centre for workshopping the final draft of the script and to Chapelle Jaffe for her superb dramaturgical feedback.

The Chilean Housing Co-op in Vancouver also provided free creation and performance space for the Latino Group for five years. Eternal gratitude for all the Chilean Housing Co-op does for Vancouver's Latinx community.

I would like to thank the Latino Theatre Group for their awe-inspiring courage, commitment, humour, and enthusiasm, and the Vancouver Latinx community for their support.

I would like to thank my family and friends for always being there.

photo: Alejandra Aguirre

Carmen Aguirre has written and co-written twenty-five plays, including *Blue Box, The Trigger,* and *The Refugee Hotel.* She is currently touring her latest one-woman show, *Broken Tailbone,* and writing three new plays: an original script entitled *Anywhere But Here,* an adaptation of Euripides's *Medea,* and an adaptation of Molière's *The Learned Ladies.* Her second memoir, *Mexican Hooker #1 and My Other Roles Since the Revolution,* published in April 2016 to outstanding reviews and shortlisted for the Hubert Evans Non-Fiction Prize, is a *Globe and Mail* bestseller and a *National Post* and CBC Best Book of 2016. Her first book, the critically acclaimed *Something Fierce: Memoirs of a Revolutionary Daughter,* won CBC Canada Reads 2012 and is a number one national bestseller. Carmen is the recipient of the Hispanic Business Alliance's 2014 Ten Most Influential Hispanics in Canada Award, Latincouver's 2014 Most Inspirational Latin Award, the 2014 Betty Mitchell Outstanding Actor Award for her work in Alberta Theatre Projects' *The Motherfucker with the Hat,* the 2012 Langara College Outstanding Alumna Award, the 2011 Union of B.C. Performers' Lorena Gale Woman of Distinction Award, and the 2002 New Play Centre Award for Best New Play for *The Refugee Hotel.* Carmen has over eighty film, TV, and stage-acting credits. She is currently starring in the independent feature *Bella Ciao!* She is a graduate of Studio 58. For more information, visit carmenaguirre.ca.